D0108967

THE END

is just the

BEGINNING

Lessons in Grieving
for African Americans

Rev. Dr. Arlene H. Churn

HARLEM MOON
BROADWAY BOOKS
NEW YORK

Harlem Moon titles may be purchased for business or promotional use or for special sales. For information, please write to: Special Markets Department, Random House, Inc., 1745 Broadway, New York, NY 10019.

PRINTED IN THE UNITED STATES OF AMERICA

The figure in the Harlem Moon logo is inspired by a graphic design by Aaron Douglas (1899–1979). HARLEM MOON and its logo, depicting a moon and woman, are trademarks of Broadway Books, a division of Random House, Inc.

"No Understanding" by Chenise Lytrelle, from the book *Life's Lessons,* published with permission of the author.

"A Child Is Loaned" adapted from the poem "To All Parents" by Edgar Guest, from the book *All in a Lifetime* © Ayer Company Publishers. Reprinted with permission.

"Peace" by Langston Hughes, from *The Collected Poems of Langston Hughes* by Langston Hughes © 1994 by The Estate of Langston Hughes. Used by permission of Alfred A. Knopf, a division of Random House, Inc.

Visit our website at www.harlemmoon.com

First edition

Book design by Donna Sinisgalli

Library of Congress Cataloging-in-Publication Data
Churn, Arlene H.
The end is just the beginning: lessons in grieving for African Americans / Arlene H. Churn.—1st ed.
p. cm.
1. Grief. 2. Bereavement—Psychological aspects. 3. Death—Psychological aspects. 4. Loss (Psychology) 5. African Americans—Psychology. I. Title.

BF575.G7 C48 2003
155.9'37'08996073—dc21   2002024104

ISBN 0-7679-1015-X

10 9 8 7 6 5 4 3 2 1

To the Memory of my Beloved Grandmother,

Wilheminia Montgomery,

And my Mother,

Theresa Harris

To My Son, Lenord Arlen Churn,

And to Delores Adrene Rush

In memory of Dr. Stacy Pierce,

Who was the inspiration for this book

Blessed Are They That Mourn

For They Shall Be Comforted

ST. MATTHEW 5:4

In glancing over my life, I was amazed to see how much death is a part of living and how it has brought so many lives together. *The End Is Just the Beginning* was written out of a need for people to understand and respect the African American perspective on death.

It is in that context that I took on the awesome task of being "the voice" for telling the story of life, death, living, and dying according to the dictates of our intricate and often misunderstood traditions.

The writing of this book was made possible through a small network of wonderful women, black and white, all of whom share a passion for reading and the written word.

I am so grateful to the Lowenstein-Morel Agency and its president, Barbara Lowenstein, who, at our first meeting, simply said, "Why don't you write a book?" She offered (and delivered on her promise) to provide me with representation and direction. Her business partner, Madeleine Morel, has been a source of silent strength (with a charming British accent) throughout the entire project. My profound thanks are extended to Janet Hill, Executive Editor of Doubleday/Harlem Moon, who saw the need for this book and made it happen. My life is richer for having been introduced to Judy Kern who, in my opinion, is America's best literary editor. Judy tolerated my late night calls, e-mails, faxes, and frustrations without ever voicing a complaint. My visits to her home were wonderful experiences, thanks to the presence and barking of her two pet dogs, Maxine and Gracie, who are now my favorite canine friends.

Thanks also to my administrative assistant, Delores Rush, my wonderful, loyal friend and confidant, who is just a bunch of blessings in my life. I am also thankful for Dr. Teressa V. Staten who, in addition to allowing me to share her story, is a dear and valued friend; to Dr. Betty Martin-Blount, who served as a tremendous resource assistant and who shared her expertise and counseling experiences. She is indeed a seasoned mentor and a true friend.

I am also grateful for the ongoing words of encouragement from my beloved pastor, the Reverend Dwight M. Jackson, and my church family at the Amity Baptist Church in Jamaica, New York; also to the Reverend Lincoln Montgomery, his wife, Ann, and the Sisterhood of the Tabernacle

Baptist Church of Wichita, Kansas; to my spiritual son, Dr. Kenneth L. Samuel, pastor of Victory Baptist Church in Stone Mountain, Georgia; and Dr. A. J. McMichael, pastor of Mt. Nebo Baptist Church in Atlanta, Georgia; to the Cathedral of Faith Baptist Church family of Camden, New Jersey, whom I served as pastor for seventeen years; and special thanks to Thelma Brown, Joyce Fowler, and Lorraine Smith, who were the wind beneath my wings.

Thank you to my special friends in ministry who prayed for me: Bishop André Jackson, pastor of New Vision Baptist Church, East Orange, New Jersey; the Reverend Kenneth D. R. Clayton, pastor of St. Luke Baptist Church, Paterson, New Jersey; and the Reverend Theo D. Spencer, pastor of Union Baptist Church, Trenton, New Jersey.

Thanks to my friend, Thomas Whitfield, of Los Angeles, California, who is associated with the Miss America Pageant, for telling me, "One day you will write a book," and for believing in my ability to do so. And to my friend of a quarter century, Douglas Holmes, retired Chief of Police, Camden, New Jersey.

This book would not have been possible without the case histories and experiences of countless clients and parishioners who allowed me to share their endings and new beginnings. Much care has been taken to mask specific identities, but each story is a true story, and each ending commenced with a new beginning.

A special thanks to my personal poet and talented goddaughter, Chenise Lytrelle Williams, and to my special godchildren, the Reverend Grant Collins, Christine Barnes, Juanita Bryant, and the Reverend Joseph Jackson, who bless my life with energizing enthusiasm and love. A lot of love to my only sister, Willida Harris Luff, who endured growing up with me and who is the sweetest of the sweet.

And finally, to my beloved son, Lenord, my thanks for your unwavering love and support, and for the joy of being your mom!

CONTENTS

Introduction

Although many books have been written on the subject of death and dying, and particularly on the process of grieving, few if any have been written by blacks specifically for the African American community. Because the experience of facing the passing of a loved one is so personal and traumatic, I believe we need to recognize the fact that people of color respond to death from a specific cultural perspective. We need to address the significant cultural differences between the ways African Americans and people of other ethnic backgrounds think about death and the manner in which it is appropriate or inappropriate to grieve. Just as people of Jewish heritage have one particular, codified set of rituals for burial and mourning, and those of Irish Catholic descent, for example, have another, African Americans' unique manner of dealing with death and mourning results from deep-seated traditions handed down through generations, since the times of slavery.

The need for this book was brought home to me most forcefully in the midst of my writing, by the tragedy of September 11, 2001. In that time of national mourning, all Americans came together, with racial, ethnic, and religious differences forgotten. But the fact remains, as reported in the *Washington Post*, that a surprisingly overwhelming percentage of those who died in the attack on the Pentagon were black. I don't know how many African Americans died in the World Trade Center, but surely the numbers were large. And one particular black hero of that day remains virtually anonymous to the American public; he was thirtysixyearold LeRoy Homer, copilot of Flight 93, which crashed near Pittsburgh, Pennsylvania. With so many of our brothers and sisters lost on that day, our community was grieving—certainly along with the rest of America, but also in our own way and for our own people.

AFRICAN AMERICANS are now coming to the realization that death is a part of life and that grieving is a natural reaction to the loss of a loved one. However, many blacks still need to understand that grief comes in many guises and that no one kind of loss is more or less worthy of grief than any other. Only the one who is grieving can fully understand the nature and extent of his or her own feelings, and, if for no other reason than that, we all must learn to look with compassion and patience upon the grief of others, even if we ourselves do not share those feelings. While many "experts" have looked at the specific, codified, and predictable "stages" of grief, I have chosen to reflect instead upon different kinds of grief because not all deaths are alike, and my experience over many years counseling thousands of grievers has taught me that not all mourning follows the same path or trajectory.

AS A CHILD of about five growing up in Philadelphia, I first became acquainted with grief when my cat died and my little heart broke. I buried him in the backyard and insisted that my playmates on the block attend the funeral. I missed him very much, for he had been the keeper of my childhood secrets and had let it be known that I was his favorite in the family. My mother and grandmother found my grief for Tommy the cat somewhat amusing, but I recall it as the first truly traumatic experience in my life.

The death of my loving and devoted grandmother was certainly the next. I was thirteen years old at the time, and it was for me a life-altering experience. In my mind, my grandmother had excelled at virtually everything she did and had made our home a neighborhood showcase. In addition to her worldly pursuits she had been very active in her church, and she always attributed all her success to the grace of God.

She was petite, powerful, successful, and spiritual, and everyone who knew us understood that she loved me with all her heart. We planned my future together, and she was my motivation to excel. She counseled me about the problems I would face as an adult, and, although I didn't always understand, I listened intently.

I recall her coming home after a medical checkup one day and announcing that she had diabetes, in addition to which her doctors had discovered a malignant tumor in her female organs. Still, she believed that her faith and her doctors would see her through. She never thought of dying because, after all, she had to live to see me grow up, and I shared in her belief.

She was hospitalized several times over the next four months, and although in those years children were not generally allowed to visit in hospitals, I was somehow a frequent visitor to her room. We continued to plan and talk as if she would be around forever, but on a stifling August day, while I was left in the care of a relative, she died. I swear to this day, I knew the moment it happened, although I wasn't told for several hours after her passing.

Feelings of disbelief, anger, fear, loneliness, madness, and confusion descended upon me at once, and I wanted to die, too. I refused to go to sleep, and the very thought of food turned my stomach. No one understood my turmoil, and some friends and relatives simply thought my "carrying on," as they put it, was totally obnoxious. As a result, I simply learned to cry in private. I had no one to talk to about my overwhelming emotions, no one to whom I could express my anger, and no one I could blame. Perhaps worst of all, there was no one to tell me how long the pain would last. I had lost the security of our special love and understanding, and, even though I had been aware of my grandmother's illness, I was confused about the reason for her death. Somehow I had thought because she was such a good and giving person that she would be granted a long life.

With her death, I lost the joy of childhood and felt guilty every time I caught myself about to experience a moment of pleasure. And I vowed never to allow anyone or anything to cause me that kind of pain again. I was insulating myself, or so I thought, from emotional pain, but I was also becoming isolated from reality.

Grief, I now understand, is an emotion that must be processed over time, and the road to healing is sometimes long and lonely. (Remember the old slave chant that moans, "Nobody knows de troubles I seen, nobody knows . . .") As a minister and pastor, I've found that we as a people rely heavily upon spiritual support in our times of grief, and that seeing death in a biblical context is often beneficial to the healing process. Luckily, there is now professional help available specifically for African Americans—including grief counseling, therapy, support groups, pastoral counseling if one is religious, and reading material. But in the end, it is often necessary to just stop and look within oneself to find relief from this very personal sorrow.

LONG BEFORE ethnic scholars began sophisticated analyses of African American culture, when the majority of blacks lived in segregated rural communities, the loss of a loved one was mourned by the community at large. This view of death as a communal loss was brought over by slaves from Africa and continued in the New World.

In Africa, the dead were revered and no expense was spared in their honor. Burial plots were often more expensive than an earthly residence, and graves were looked upon as hallowed ground by the entire tribe.

In the New World, we remain a people that is emotionally connected, and we naturally join in public expressions of grief and bereavement because we understand that sharing the mourners' grief can make it easier for the survivors to cope with their loss. Unfortunately, however, during the years of slavery, masters were uncomfortable with and fearful of their slaves' primitive, mystical traditions, most often forbidding their slaves the opportunity for either public mourning or private grieving. Denied the privilege of land ownership for burial and the freedom to perform their tribal rituals for celebrating the dead, enslaved blacks were forced to mourn in a different manner. They became creative in their grieving, learning to shed silent tears and moan chants of comfort quietly to themselves and with each other.

It was this generation that embraced wholeheartedly the concept of a heavenly home, with its promise of transformation and reunion with friends and family on the other side. In fact, it could be said that these enslaved mourners were really grieving for themselves, because they were still living in slavery while the deceased had been "freed" by death.

They grieved for loved ones who had died in a lynching, who'd been beaten to death, or who had been left to die "like a dog" without adequate medical attention. In the eyes of their masters, slaves were interchangeable commodities, but for those they left behind, the loss was irreplaceable and deeply felt. Sadly and ironically, it must be noted that today many African Americans are once again mourning untimely deaths, this time resulting from murder, car accidents, gang warfare, and other forms of violence.

IN LATER YEARS, African Americans adopted biblical guidelines for mourning. Weeping was justified because "Jesus wept" over the death of his friend Lazarus (John 11:35, King James Version), and, according to scripture, when Christ died on the cross, the whole earth grieved and mourned his passing: "And it was about the sixth hour, and there was a darkness over all the earth until the ninth hour. And the sun was darkened, and the veil of the temple was rent in the midst." (Luke 23:44–45, KJV) "And all the people that came together to that sight . . . smote their breasts . . ." (Luke 23:48, KJV) In other words, when He died, the people cried and were demonstrative in their grieving.

We African Americans gain a degree of relief when we

can display our grief in dramatic ways, such as sobbing, screaming, fainting, even throwing ourselves on the open coffin during the funeral. And one might speculate that such extreme demonstrations, as well as other extravagances, are cultural reactions to the interdictions placed on overt mourning during the years of slavery.

These days, we don't simply have funerals, we have "celebration of life" services or "victory" services, services of "elevation" or "transition" or "home-going." Whites who attend black funerals are sometimes amazed and confused by the elaborate "final arrangements." It's not unusual for the service to last three to five hours, including many songs, lengthy "remarks," and an almost endless reading of the resolutions and sympathy cards sent in honor of the deceased. Although it's no longer mandatory that families adhere to a uniform dress code, relatives still proceed into the room according to their "rank" or the closeness of their relationship to the one who has passed. Even the printed programs are creative works of art, often including several pages of photos depicting the life of the departed from "alpha" to "omega" or "sunrise" to "sunset," as the dates of birth and death are sometimes designated. The notion that the deceased is actually able to hear the many accolades and declarations of love and affection being heaped upon him, or to witness the sacrifices being made for his elaborate "home-going," is reinforced by printed poems or verses like the one that follows, which purport to reflect his or her sentiments.

> I'd like the memory of me to be a happy one.
> I'd like to leave an afterglow of smiles
> When life is done.
> I'd like the tears of those who grieve
> To dry before the sun
> Of happy memories that I leave
> When life on earth is done.

Smiles shine through tears when family members are told that their loved one "would have been so pleased with everything." "Well, I did the best I could," the person in charge is likely to reply, with self-deprecating, if not entirely genuine humility.

Finally, one of the most important aspects of that last good-bye for black people is the viewing of the remains, a custom that also finds its origin in scripture. When Thomas, a beloved disciple of Christ, was informed of the resurrection, he told his fellow disciples that "Except I shall see in his hands the print of the nails, and put my finger into the print of the nails, and thrust my hand into his side, I will not believe." (John 21:25, KJV) For modern "doubting Thomases" in the African American community, viewing the body brings closure and acceptance of the finality of death, as well as the opportunity to properly pay their last respects. Although Catholic churches have always prohibited any public viewing of the remains within the church, it is common practice in African American churches to view the body twice—once before the start of the "order of service" and again at the conclusion. I've even known families to change the location of the service when they learn that the church they have chosen no longer allows what they consider to be this final opportunity to bid their loved one farewell. For many blacks, actually looking upon the dead is a way to process the understanding that he or she is truly gone, and so to begin a healthy period of active mourning.

"I ALMOST died laughing" or "My feet are killing me" or "You almost scared me to death" are off-the-cuff remarks we African Americans make every day without ever thinking about the somber truths that lie behind these colloquialisms. But when death actually arrives, it brings with it a constellation of mixed emotions. Survivors might be mad, sad, or even glad. They might be mad because they think the deceased "just gave up," sad because, in their opinion, the one who died "had everything to live for," or simply glad that a loved one is no longer suffering.

We all live in stressful times, but for many of us the stress of everyday life is amplified by worry over finances and the ability to provide for our families. And, unfortunately, stress can lead not only to compromised health—even death—but it can also be transferred to those who are left behind. When the simple stress of adjusting to life without the deceased is compounded by very real socioeconomic concerns, the mourner can become hopeless, helpless, fearful, and, therefore, unable to recover from grief and resume normal activities.

Another prevalent source of stress among grievers is the "mess" the deceased often leaves as his or her legacy. Even when there were no "money worries" while the loved one was alive, bills or other obligations of which the family knows nothing and the absence of sufficient financial provision made for the primary survivor can lead to frustration and anger that hamper the ability of the living to grieve for the dead.

Many a mourner has tearfully wondered in frustration, "How could he do this to me? Just look at the mess he left behind," as he or she focuses on the "unfinished business" rather than the loss of the deceased. When these negative emotions become the griever's primary connection to a loved one who has passed, they leave a "bitter taste in the mouth" that can sorely impede the process of recovery. The mourner might actually shut down emotionally, vow never to trust another person again, and thus fail to develop the new attachments that are a necessary part of beginning again. And if family members argue about the details of what their loved one failed to do, those quarrels can actually break down the existing bonds that are so necessary for finding emotional support in times of need. We need to remember that the living should never argue over the dead. But we must also take to heart the Lord's admonishment to Hezekiah in Isaiah 38:1 (KJV): "Set thine house in order: for thou shalt die, and not live."

OUR FAILURE so often to set our house in order is but one manifestation of our reluctance to admit that there won't always be another tomorrow. We'd prefer to assume there will always be more time to share with our loved ones, to visit, or just to stay in touch, and as a result, we sometimes take our loved ones for granted. Particularly now, schedules can be so demanding and lifestyles so complicated that families are no longer bonded as they once were. The close-knit African American family structure has undergone a radical change. Elders are no longer revered as matriarchs and patriarchs; grandparents are no longer cared for at home as a matter of course; and younger family members don't always visit on a regular basis. This kind of inadvertent neglect can also lead to guilt and remorse when an elder relative dies and we realize that we'll no longer have the opportunity to make amends.

This can be particularly difficult for young blacks who, regrettably, are losing the deeply imbedded belief and faith in God that has been the source of strength for African Americans in trying times, going back to the days of slavery. Too often our young people now believe that they're prepared for whatever life will bring and deny the need to rely on an unseen deity. When faced with the unexpected death of a loved one, however, their self-reliance often fails them miserably and they vent their negative emotions upon the "god" they don't believe in. Without the faith that sustained so many generations before them, it's sometimes difficult for these young people to work through their anger, guilt, or remorse and to focus on a productive future for themselves.

Having so often seen this happen, I value even more the legacy left to me by my grandmother. She not only taught me to have faith in myself, but also instilled in me a deep faith that all things are possible and that God would guide me toward doors and windows of opportunity, helping me to achieve whatever goals I set for myself. It's that faith that guides me to this day, as I go about my ministerial duties and in all aspects of my personal life.

Like all little children, I loved being read to at bedtime, and I particularly remember one story my grandmother returned to again and again, of the little blue train struggling to carry its cargo over the mountain and repeating over and over, "I think I can, I think I can." And then, as it reached the peak and started down the other side, "I thought I could, I thought I could." My beloved grandmother possessed not only an abiding faith in God, but also a deep belief in the power of positive thinking. "Believe and you will receive" was her constant admonition to me, and, in later years, I came to discover that, indeed, even a small fragment of faith can move mountains. "If ye have faith," Jesus told the multitudes, "as a grain of a mustard seed... nothing shall be impossible unto you." (Matt. 17:20, KJV)

If our faith is firmly in place, I believe, it will not be shaken even by death, but will act as the rock and foundation upon which we can build a new life. As a minister, I preach that our source of comfort in all things lies in our personal relationship with God, and the foundation of my calling, both as a minister and as a therapist, derives from Isaiah 61:1–3 (KJV).

> The spirit of the Lord God is upon me; because the Lord hath anointed me to preach good tidings unto the meek; he hath sent me to bind up the broken‑hearted, to proclaim liberty to the captives, and the opening of the prison to them that are bound; to proclaim the acceptable year of the Lord, and the day of vengeance of our God; to comfort all who mourn; to appoint unto them that mourn in Zion, to give unto them beauty for ashes, the oil of joy for mourning, the garment of praise for the spirit of heaviness: that they might be called trees of righ‑teousness, the planting of the Lord, that he might be glorified.

As a people, we have long been taught that both the gift of life and the sting of death are solely "in the hands of God." But with that in mind, we must also remember that death is not a divine punishment but rather a part of life. It is the bridge from this world to the spiritual realm.

In Psalm 90:9 (KJV), David sums up life by saying "We spend our years as a tale that is told." Each life is a story with a beginning, a middle, and an end, and, naturally, the end is mourned by those who are left behind. But we should never grieve without gratitude for the life of the departed, and must always bear in mind that we live by the grace of God, whose exclusive power over life and death is acknowledged when, during the burial ritual, the minister quotes the summary of life with the words "earth to earth, ashes to ashes, and dust to dust." The physical body returns to the earth, whence it came, and the spirit returns to God to live eternally, liberated from this earthly life.

I cherish my childhood memories of the "old black saints" who used to "testify" in church about their anticipation of "going home to be with the Lord." They summed up their lives as "living to live again," and gloried in their visions of white robes, sparkling crowns, streets of gold, sitting around God's throne, and singing in the heavenly choir. They spoke unashamedly of being tired and weary of this life and of looking forward to the promised "peace in the valley" that lay ahead. They promised mourners that "God will wipe away all tears" and comforted those who feared the future without their loved one with the assurance that "He didn't bring you this far to leave you." And how I loved to hear them say that "in that great gettin' up mornin', ain't no grave gonna hold my body down."

• • •

ALTHOUGH, PERSONALLY, I'm glad the decision as to when and how to die is not left up to individual choice; for some, the death of a loved one reveals for the first time their own lack of control as well as their own vulnerability. For the first time, they are forced to look their own mortality in the face, and that can be a frightening experience. For too many African Americans, it is an insight that can result in an unproductive kind of grieving for something they don't understand, which then prevents them from moving on with their lives. But we all need to confront the reality of our own demise sooner or later, and to understand that we are all temporary residents on this plane. Particularly in difficult times, we need to reconnect to the legacy of faith that has sustained our people for so many years, and ask for the strength we will need not only to get through today but also to face our tomorrows.

Eulogies in the African American tradition usually consist of exhortations from the Bible, words of comfort, and a warning to those in attendance to get ready, for "you know not the day or the hour when you are to appear before the judgment throne of God." The service is followed by the trek to the cemetery, the burial commitment at the grave, the placing of flowers on the casket, hugs and kisses, food and fellowship, and then the farewells of friends and relatives with exhortations to "call me if you need me."

The ceremonies are over, but the grieving process is just about to begin as the reality and finality of the loss finally sinks in. Grief may cause temporary—and sometimes permanent—changes in behavior, thoughts, dreams, and goals. But what the mourner must always keep in mind is that, regardless of the pain, he or she must adapt to the world of the present and not continue to reside in the life of the dead.

These pages are full of the stories and experiences of people who have crossed my path as a minister and grief counselor and who have made it through the turbulence of grieving. Despite detours and setbacks, these people have found a way to put an end to their grief and begin life anew. It is my hope that the stories of their day-to-day victories will be a source of comfort and support in difficult times to all who read this book. If you are mourning the loss of a loved one, you need to understand that, whatever your loss, you are not alone, and it is my goal to provide you with a community of those who have gone before, who have found comfort in their memories and the courage to continue living rich and fulfilling lives, because, as you, too, will discover . . . the end is just the beginning.

※

ONE

Regret and Denial

For my life is spent with grief
and my years with sighing.

PSALM 31:10a

My mother! She was my personal possession. I would never have another mother—only one biological mother per lifetime—and mine was gone, suddenly, at the age of fifty-six, the result of a medical mishap. She had gone into the hospital for the removal of a small growth on her gum, so that her dentures would fit properly. Yet, for reasons unknown, she went into cardiac arrest and lay in a coma for nine days.

From Washington, D.C., where I was living at the time, I rushed to her bedside in Philadelphia and stayed there around the clock, praying for a miracle of healing and the restoration of health. And while I prayed, I also reflected on the years following the death of my grandmother, during which the relationship between my mother and me had been so strained.

My mother, Theresa, had been a young widow with two little girls to raise on her own when my grandmother insisted that we come to live with her. At that point, Grandmother took total charge and control of our lives. My mother was her only child and she looked upon all three of us as "her girls." As a result, my mother had always felt she'd been denied the opportunity to raise her daughters as she saw fit, and my grandmother, on her part, had always felt that her daughter lacked what we now call "parenting skills." Grandmother provided us with a wonderful lifestyle and never begrudged us anything. However, she was disappointed that my mother chose not to be involved in the businesses she had established—her beauty school and rental properties. I, on the other hand, was in awe of all my grandmother did, and I became her little partner. She was my best friend and my playmate. I was with her constantly, and my mother knew enough not to interfere with our special relationship and bond.

Now, while maintaining my bedside vigil, I thought about our past lack of appreciation for each other's individuality. I had wanted my mother to be like my grandmother, who was strong and assertive and who transformed the impossible dream for an African American woman into a vision of reality. She was successful in business and had a passion for motivating others to chart their own life's course on the path of excellence. She refused to accept limitations based on gender or race, and she willingly accepted being misunderstood and misjudged as the price she had to pay for her success. My grandmother was generous to a fault and never complained, even when she was taken advantage of, because she believed strongly that if your heart is in the right place, the giver is never the loser.

My mother was completely different. Soft-spoken, meek, and humorous, she held no high aspirations for her life. "Just live and let live" was her motto. She enjoyed her friends and the things they did together—weekly card games, going to weekend dances, and simply having good, clean fun. And she never really understood the lasting impact my grandmother had made on my life. She didn't know about the countless conversations we'd had, during which my grandmother had encouraged me to accept life's challenge to exceed society's expectations and the limitations it placed on Negro women. Grandmother never rewarded me for being on the honor roll because my achievement was no more than she'd expected, yet she was proud of me and enjoyed boasting about my grades and school honors to anyone who would listen.

At an early age, I felt the call to be a minister. I wanted to be an articulate female proclaimer in ministry. My mother was appalled by this choice, but my grandmother was thrilled for me. She prayed with me and gave me guidance, encouragement, and support. She also tried to prepare me for the obstacles I'd face if I pursued this calling, and insisted that I get as much education as possible. She told me I could succeed at my chosen vocation even in a male-dominated field. With her encouragement, understanding, and unconditional love, I was able to endure rejection and ridicule and become a pioneer in the field for African American women, gaining respect, acceptance, and national recognition within the religious community.

After college, I married a career military officer several years my senior, and my mother loved him dearly. She saw security and stability for me in this marriage. On Valentine's Day, 1964, our beautiful son, Lenord, was born, and becoming a "nana" changed my mother's life as she strove to be the best nana in the world.

My marriage ended when my son was seventeen months old, and that was when my mother truly became my mother in every sense of the word. For the first time, we were able to talk openly and gain insight into each other's lives, dreams and goals, successes and failures. I cried when she told me how proud she was of my accomplishments and how much she admired me for pursuing my academic and ministerial goals.

So now, while maintaining my vigil at her bedside, I prayed, I cried, and I talked to her incessantly. I begged her to open her eyes, wiggle a toe, make a sound, but she never responded. At 3:05 A.M. on November 19, 1967, she died.

REGRET

Regret has many faces and many meanings. Those who have lost a loved one may regret acts left unperformed or words unspoken. We may regret the loss to ourselves of someone who loved and supported us unconditionally. And our friends and relatives may regret that we have been so saddened and are suffering such a loss. It is an emotion involving sorrow and remorse, and one that often demands some act of penitence.

My own regrets when my mother died were too numerous to list here. I began by regretting not having taken trips with her, not exchanging advice about things that were important to each of us. I felt deep sorrow and painful remorse.

Our act of penitence is often carried out as some form of ongoing after-death apology. For example, we African

Americans are known to be extremely vocal at funerals, frequently moaning, "I'm sorry" and "Please forgive me." As a form of penitence, some people begin to perform acts they know would have pleased the departed. They might start to attend church regularly (at least for a while), return to school, or participate in family activities—all to make up for not having done these things while the deceased was alive. In the same way, others might give up behaviors they know displeased their loved one. Either way, the mourner may derive a small sense of comfort from believing that the departed would be pleased or proud of his or her effort to make up and be forgiven for past conduct.

Often we hear grievers lament, "If I had only known"— which means, of course, they really did know—of deeds left undone and acts of kindness they could have bestowed upon the deceased. Certainly that was true in my case.

THE MANNER or cause of our loved one's death can sometimes delay our regret. In the case of a severe and prolonged illness, for example, we might first feel relief, followed by regret. But the manner of death—alone, after prolonged suffering, or as the result of an accident or violent crime—can also be a cause of regret, as can the age of the deceased. Our regret is always that much greater when someone dies young or in the prime of life. But, life is a gift and death is a given. How and when we die is but a small part of the mystery of life, known only to the Creator, the giver of life, and we must, therefore, learn to live through the "could have/should have" phase of mourning and move on to the realization that there is no way to undo or redo the past. All we can do is forgive ourselves, adopt a new attitude about life in general, and begin to cherish each day as a new beginning.

IN GROUP therapy sessions, many people confess that what they really regret is that they no longer have their loved one physically available to them. Simply put, just knowing and accepting the reality that the deceased is no longer "there for me," is the one regret they find most difficult to overcome. In this sense, their regret is actually for themselves rather than for the deceased.

This is particularly true for African Americans, as we have always drawn strength from close family ties and deep, established relationships. Perhaps because of racism and other social divisions, we have looked within the circle of family and special friends for our main source of strength and security. We habitually pledge to "always be there" for someone we love. Even the lyrics of a popular song recorded in the 1960s by The Four Tops have led us to believe that "If ever you need me, I'll be there," and often we take that pledge literally, which makes it all the harder for us to accept the fact that when a loved one dies neither we nor the deceased can continue to keep that promise. And the broken pledge can also be a two-edged sword, because if someone has vowed to "always be there" for us, we in turn may come to feel that he or she is our possession—my husband, my wife, my baby, my home girl, my main man, my woman. If we interpret that to mean "mine and mine alone," the loss can leave a permanent, unfillable void.

ONE OF the strengths of African American culture is that we can always find solace in a song, scripture, or an old saying handed down to us by elders who have weathered similar personal storms. Before there were support groups, therapy, and counseling, we gained strength and healing from songs. And these simple chants still provide temporary comfort and postpone the need for an immediate answer to our questions.

"Why and why now?" is the question answered in the song "We'll Understand It Better By and By," while the lament "How am I going to make it?" finds a response in the song "God Will Take Care of You." In these and other verses, we are admonished to accept the will of God because He makes no mistakes, and, at the same time, we are assured that "He will be a mother for the motherless, a father for the fatherless, and a friend that will stick closer than a brother"—words that are intended to relieve us of feeling any regret for the loss.

SOOTHING WORDS of Old Testament scripture can almost always be found in Psalm 23, "The Lord Is My Shepherd," which reassures us that "Yea, though I walk through the valley of the shadow of death, I will fear no evil, for Thou art with me . . ." God, the psalm tells us, will be with the griever in this dark hour, and He will also accompany the deceased on his journey of passage from life to death.

The New Testament scripture of comfort is usually John 14, verses 1 to 3, which promise grievers and mourners that the departed is going to a better place where he will reside with God until such time as they are all reunited on the other side:

Let not your Heart be troubled,

Ye believe in God, believe also in Me,

In my Father's house are many mansions,

If it were not so, I would have told you,

I go to prepare a place for you, that where

I am, there ye may be also.

ONCE THE songs are sung and the scripture read, however, re‑
gret for the loss of a loved one still remains with the griever,
and too often, in our effort to postpone the inevitable feeling
of emptiness, we resort to denial as a way of dealing with our
regret.

DENIAL

In our community, both regret and denial are often expressed
through elaborate funerals and floral displays, expensive cas‑
kets, numerous limos, even color‑coordinated outfits for the
immediate family. Such extravagances are intended as state‑
ments of love and esteem for the deceased, as if he or she
were aware of the display (or the extent of the family's grief).

In recent years, African American culture has accepted

a redefinition of death as no longer permanent and final, but rather a temporary absence or transformation of the deceased into a spiritual being who has ongoing knowledge of earthly affairs. Our people have a long history of wanting to communicate with the dead. Often it is out of simple curiosity, or because they need to know where the deceased is in the afterworld. Still others seek confirmation that their loved one is happy on the "other side," enjoying the fellowship of others who passed before him. And finally, there are those who desperately seek direction for their own lives through communication with the dead.

This is a delicate stage of grieving, when the griever must use caution in order to avoid being taken advantage of by those who prey upon and profit from other people's frantic grief. In the film *Ghost,* Whoopi Goldberg portrayed a woman who had the ability to communicate with the dead, and in real life many people invest thousands of dollars in this kind of pursuit.

One of my favorite stories brings into sharp if humorous focus the absurdity of this kind of denial. A woman whose neighbor had died arrived at the funeral with a crock of chicken soup. Some of her fellow mourners thought she was demented, while others just thought her behavior was downright embarrassing. But, when reminded that she was, in fact, at a funeral, the woman replied, "If she can see and smell those flowers, she can eat this soup."

Amusing as this story may be, it accurately reflects the fact that many African Americans do enter a state of denial, partly as a way to assuage their regret and partly just to deny the inevitable reality of death. A much-quoted verse from a poem by Helen Steiner Rice validates this sentiment when it says "they are just away," implying that they may some day return. But describing death as an unexplained or temporary absence only serves to reinforce unhealthy denial of the truth.

FOR AFRICAN Americans, this tendency toward denial is often encouraged by the abundance of food, fun, and fellowship that has always provided an opportunity for escape and retreat from reality during the grieving period.

In contrast with other ethnic or religious groups—such as those of the Jewish faith, who traditionally bury their dead within twenty-four hours—African Americans often schedule their funerals for the convenience of relatives or loved ones who must travel long distances to attend, which means that there can be a lapse of anywhere from five to eight days between the death and the burial. In the interim, food and more food is carried to the family home as more and more people arrive. Old photographs might be brought out and passed around, generating laughter and wistful smiles. And you can bet that someone will have a "do you remember" or a "how about the time" story that will inevitably be subject to correction by others who recall the incident differently.

During this period, the family is showered with affection and attention, which often leads to a delay in their acceptance of death as a permanent state. Denial takes on a life of its own, and for some it evolves into an unhealthy way of dealing with their loss. It becomes too easy to think of the loved one as simply being "in another room," as one griever described this period to me.

THE FINALITY of death was easier for us to accept when a wreath adorned the door of the family residence, as was the custom until the early 1970s, and all mourners wore black (the immediate family for a period of thirty days) as a display of their bereavement. All forms of levity were taboo during this time, and there was no doubt that a death had occurred. Death was doleful, and funerals were sad, for it was understood that this was the end of a life.

In recent times, however, the dead are referred to simply

as "the departed," or "asleep in Jesus." And denial is made easier by the well-meaning assurances of friends and associates that we will see our lost loved one again.

The degree to which such euphemisms and false assurances can lead to unhealthy denial was brought home to me in a grief therapy session involving minors. These children had been led to believe that their loved one was just asleep in the casket and had begun to experience nightmares during which the deceased awoke after being buried under six feet of dirt. Although it is certainly well meant, adult denial should never be passed on to children, and death should be explained to them at their own level of understanding.

Sadly, the African American community is now coping with a generation of young mourners who see death occur all too frequently as the result of neighborhood violence, drugs, gang killings, and drive-by shootings. Children are seeing children die more than ever in our recorded history, and they are writing a new chapter in African American grieving as they mourn the death of their peers. Often the drama of death is overwhelming and confusing to children because they are introduced to it so suddenly, with no time for adequate "preparation." Young children often ask, "When is he coming back?" and sometimes they've been known to demand that the dead "wake up."

When children are denied the opportunity to attend a funeral (because they are deemed "too young to understand") or are not allowed to participate in the planning, being left out of the process can sometimes add to their confusion and prevent them from accepting death as a final and permanent state. A child may be told "he's gone" or "she's gone," but no one gives the child the rest of the story. Gone where? For how long? And when will he—or she—be back? Inquiring little minds want the answers to these questions.

Many people think children are too young to understand death, but I disagree. I believe that at whatever age a child experiences love, he or she is also capable of feeling loss, and that feeling leaves the child with an unexplained emptiness and a longing to fill that space in his life.

I CAN personally attest, from my own experience, to the insidious power of denial as a coping mechanism. My mother was buried the Tuesday before Thanksgiving. The funeral was beautiful. The church was wreathed in flowers and overflowing with people. The service was dignified and without excessive drama. I was hugged, I cried, beautiful words were spoken, and the music was awesome. The repast hour at the church following the burial was a small banquet, it seemed. And when it was over, I immediately returned to Washington.

On Thanksgiving morning, my first thought was to call my mother and wish her a happy holiday. But as soon as I touched the phone, I was reminded of the brutal fact that my mother was dead and that I had heard her voice for the last time. I then realized that I'd gone those several days in total denial. I'd tried to convince myself that she was still in Philadelphia, but now I was forced to accept the reality of her permanent absence from my life. After that realization, I was in both physical and spiritual pain for an extended period of time. And the most difficult lesson I had to learn was that pain is part of the healing process. So long as we do not experience pain, we are in denial of our loss, for we must accept the permanence of that loss in order to heal and move on.

My healing began gradually as I learned to observe an emotional anniversary in celebration of Mother's life. Someone suggested that I keep "a pile of memories" available. Tears of sorrow and sadness became tears of joy as I allowed those precious memories of good times past to flow through my mind. I learned that the spirit of our loved ones lives on within their survivors.

My permanent exit from the City of Denial came one

day when I was about to indulge in a private "pity party" about the loss of my mother and other loved ones. My administrator and dearest friend, Delores, insisted I listen to a recording by the famous blues artist, Bobby Blue Bland. I was a bit perturbed by her selection of a blues song, given my state of mind and mood at the time, but I listened, and the words of that song, "You've Got To Hurt Before You Heal," spoke to my soul. After listening to those words, I recalled an injury I'd sustained in an accident. At first it was too painful even to touch. Eventually the pain subsided, yet I still carry the scar. The pain is gone forever, but the scar remains.

So it is with the healing of grief. See the scar, relive the event, but know the pain is gone.

FOR MANY of our people, hugging is healing, and it's important that we both give and receive physical contact during our initial period of mourning. Our children, in particular, need to be held and hugged as reassurance that they're not alone. Take all the strength and comfort you can in those early days from the friends and family who surround you, and then begin to concentrate on regaining your strength and control so that you can start your new life in a different way.

Learn to appreciate the fact that your life has been enriched as a direct result of your relationship with the deceased. Learn to live in the *now*, for today is all we have and tomorrow is still an unfulfilled hope. Take that trip, buy yourself a present, visit your friends, and enjoy the gift of today as another chance to begin again.

❋

LESSONS IN HEALING

- Forgive yourself for deeds left undone and unexpressed words of kindness. You can't relive the past, but you can begin to cherish each day as a new beginning.

- Do not deny the reality of death, to yourself or to your children, for without the pain of acceptance there can be no true healing.

- Keep your precious memories alive by creating a memory box or scrapbook that you can look to for solace and take joy from the good times you enjoyed. Relive these events but know the pain has passed.

- Remember your loved one's birthdays and anniversaries, but recall that these are meant to be celebrations—not another funeral.

HEALING WORDS

Today I will maintain a calm spirit and a peaceful disposition. No matter what the test, this is my day of rest. I will not entertain outside intimidation or inner guilt about this restful retreat. This mental excursion will empower me for the tests and tasks of oncoming tomorrows, but for now, I claim this day as a day of rest from the test.

✳

Death Is a Part of Life

He is a man of sorrows and
acquainted with grief.

ISAIAH 53:3b

In the African American culture, we need to know that death and grief are part of the rhythms of life.

The Random House Dictionary defines grief as "keen mental suffering or distress over affliction or loss; sharp sorrow; painful regret." It's an emotion that must be processed over time, and the road to healing is often a long and lonely one.

Many African Americans appear to be delayed in their pursuit of healing and resolution after the death of a loved one because they don't understand that permanent closure is virtually impossible to achieve. The deceased one is never really forgotten or banished from our thoughts. As an example of our remembrance, reverence, and ongoing celebration for our dead, we have only to think of figures such as civil rights martyrs Dr. Martin Luther King, Jr., Medgar Evers, the six little girls who were burned to death in a Birmingham church in the 1960s, the revolutionary activist Malcolm X, or even the hip-hop icon Tupac Shakur.

As a people, we seem to have total recall about death. Whether the one who's gone is a close family member, a friend, or a celebrity of national prominence, we remember the day, the hour, where we were, and what we were doing at the time of the death. When we discuss the dead, words like "I remember it as if it were yesterday" or "I'll never forget it as long as I live" bring nods of acknowledgment affirming that "I know what you mean. I feel the same way."

As a group, we must learn to accept the fact that the death of a loved one is not the termination of the griever's life as well, and that the life of the survivor can be one of restored joy and fulfillment. We simply need to realize that their end is our beginning.

We have to learn how to keep moving on—through grief, mourning, and personal loss—and not move into a state of perpetual grief. Grieving for a loved one should not become all-consuming. The impact of death has caused too many people in our culture to stop living and simply exist on memories of the dead.

We must learn that there is no magic moment of closure or invisible eraser to wipe away the pain, loneliness, and bitterness. But each day is an opportunity to begin to live life without the physical presence of the deceased.

EXTENDED GRIEVING can also be an act of selfishness, for few of us invite others to share in our grief, and we often resent and refuse the efforts of other people to help us in the process of healing.

I recall one group therapy session during which a new client was very uncomfortable and left almost immediately. When I asked why she'd left, she said she'd been upset because everyone else in the group seemed to be happy! I told her they were at that stage of grief recovery when smiles and pleasantries were permissible without feeling guilty. But she indicated that she would never get to that point. I asked if she intended to go through the rest of her life without ever smiling or laughing again, and she sadly replied, "That's the way I feel right now."

Like countless others, this woman believed her life had ended with the death of her loved one, who, in this instance, was her husband.

• • •

TOO MANY people lose their personal identity in the grieving process because of the labels attached to them by society. People are called "widows" or "widowers," "childless" mothers or fathers, or "orphans," and they then too often assume those identities, the wife without a husband or the husband without a wife, becoming the bereft parents, or the motherless or fatherless child. We must never lose our sense of self or of self-worth because, regardless of the loss of a loved one, we are still somebody, and somebody who is yet alive.

We must learn to live our own life as an individual, rather than living as an extension of a deceased relative or intimate friend. It's a challenge to live without certain loved ones in our life, but it can be done.

While the deceased can never be replaced (nor should we try to replace them), we must allow room for a new beginning without them, knowing that our life has been forever blessed and enriched because of them.

"LIFE WILL never be the same" is the cry of so many grievers, but in that bitter cry lies the brutal truth that death is a part of life. Life does go on, in spite of death, disappointment, heartache, and pain. For solace, I would ask the bereaved to look to Saint Paul the Apostle who, in First Corinthians, chapter 15 (KJV), addresses death with these words: "O death, where is thy sting, O grave, where is thy victory?" I believe the message of this passage is that we should look upon death not as the victory of a mortal enemy but rather as an interruption in the flow of life.

African American elders, who were always most creative in their descriptions of the final passage, have been known to refer to death as the grim reaper arriving on a horse without a rider, or to explain the departure of a loved one as his being summoned home by God and carried away by the "death angel." When the deceased was of advanced years, it was said that his "work on earth was done," and when a child died, the family was enjoined to take comfort in the fact that "only the good die young."

In recent years, however, African Americans have begun to reject these simplistic explanations and to react to death with an outward display of their anger and disbelief.

One family with whom I worked had lost their only daughter, Monique, in a car accident that also involved the deaths of six other teenagers. Monique's mother, Dorothy, was upset because she felt, based on what she saw as their lack of extreme mourning, that no one else in the family really loved Monique. She didn't understand how her husband, Donald, could return to work so soon after the funeral, or how her son, Matthew, could resume his after-school sports activities and discuss his games without ever mentioning his sister's name.

Matthew like to play video games with his friends, and he asked that he be allowed to move from his smaller bedroom into Monique's larger room, so he'd have more space for his posters and his collection of Star Trek figures. His mother insisted, however, that the room remain exactly as it was before Monique's death. She said she felt Monique's presence in that room. She was convinced that she and her daughter communicated in that room, and she was angry that her husband and son chose not to share that experience.

Dorothy believed that each of their lives and their demeanor should be permanently altered as a result of Monique's death. She was angry that her husband could go bowling; she was upset that she never saw him cry or appear depressed, and she didn't understand how he could tell her, "You need to get over it and get on with your life." What life? To her, life had ended forever when Monique died, and that included the family's life as well.

Dorothy had stopped all her activities, including singing in the church choir and attending the meetings and functions of her social club. She refused to go anywhere except to work as a teller in a downtown bank. Her grief can be compared to that of the biblical Rachel. Jeremiah 31:15 speaks of Rachel's bitter weeping and lamentation for her children, and of her refusal to be comforted. "A voice was heard in Ramah, lamentation, and bitter weeping, Rachel weeping for her children refused to be comforted for her children, because they were not . . ." However, in verse 16 of that same chapter there is divine promise in the words "There is hope in thine end, saith the Lord."

Dorothy's entire family was in a dire state of complicated grief and mourning, because they were unable to understand each other's way of grieving. Donald returned to work and to his other activities and almost never mentioned his daughter's name. Dorothy interpreted his behavior as a lack of love for his daughter. But African American men are often pressured to be "manly" in every situation, and from early childhood many black males are told, "A man ain't supposed to cry." Boys who cry when they're hurt or embarrassed are told to "be a man," and tears are viewed as a sign of weakness both by their elders and by their peers. This misconception about displaying emotion causes many African American men to adopt a stoic façade: "I won't cry, I can handle it because I'm a man and men don't cry." Black men do grieve differently from women, yet men must learn that they also need to express their feelings and that it's okay for men to cry.

And in this case, Donald, like many African American men, needed to return to work almost immediately because of the family's financial situation. Often men in the workplace don't know how to extend comfort and support to another man, and they simply expect him to "do his job."

Donald, however, should have served as an example for his son, who needed to see him express verbal and nonverbal feelings as a man dealing with grief. Dorothy, for her part, needed to understand that her husband was grieving for their daughter in his own private way, and they both had to learn to support and encourage one another during this trying time. I counseled them to share their feelings and fears, hurt and pain.

And the family also needed to see that Matthew, like all children, was grieving in cycles. Children need the emotional relief of grieving, and then they need to do what children their age would do under normal circumstances. Both Donald and Dorothy had to be reminded that Monique's death was a new experience for them, both as a family and as individuals. Matthew had learned the harsh fact that not only the sick and elderly die, but that accidents and illness claim the lives of young people as well.

I shared with them the words of a wise old soul who once told me, "Life is a journey, and we travel on life's path until the path ends." For some it's a long journey. For others it's a short trip, but it's important to enjoy the journey at whatever pace you travel.

The family finally admitted that Monique had enjoyed life, and that when her life abruptly ended, she was with friends, all of whom came to the end of their journey together. She hadn't died alone, and the other children's families were also feeling grief and pain over the loss of their children.

THE REALIZATION of one's need and desire to overcome constant grieving is eloquently expressed in the words of Martha, one of my clients, who came into therapy because, she said, she was "sick and tired of being sick and tired."

Martha had grieved over her father's death for five long years. Becoming his caregiver after he had a stroke had become her whole life. She felt that caring for him was her reason for living, and she tried to meet his every need on a daily basis. She bathed him, fed him, and spent every waking moment she could by his side.

Martha had put her own life on hold because of her love

for her dad. She insisted that it was not a burden to care for him, and she believed he would have done the same for her. She felt she was obligated to this labor of love because of the sacrifices her father had made to ensure her education by working two jobs, which, she felt, had been the cause of his failing health.

Her mother had died when Martha was only fifteen years old, and she couldn't recall her father's ever having a date or taking a vacation without her after that. When his stroke left him paralyzed and bedridden, she vowed he would never go into a nursing facility, and she was true to her word. She learned how to inject his prescribed medication intravenously, and she had no problem diapering him when that was necessary. She did it all and never complained.

When he died, she was lost, and she discovered that at the age of thirty-nine she had forgotten how to live. Her sorrow was deep and painful, and she was in a state of despair. She had no companion or close relatives, and good girlfriends had become a thing of the past. After five years of grieving, she was tired and confused about how to start living a real life again.

Martha and others like her have to learn that life demands living until you die. They have to learn that life does go on, even in the absence of a loved one or in spite of a loss that has caused extended grief and mourning. There is your life to live after death, and the griever needs to acknowledge that death is a part of life.

ANOTHER OF my clients who needed to learn this bitter but ultimately liberating lesson, had experienced the death of a loved one under circumstances that couldn't have been more different from those of Martha and her family.

Lee was a high school teacher who had been adopted at birth by an elderly, stern, but loving couple in the rural South. He is typical of those African American children who are generally labeled "old folks' children," and who, because of the age of their parents, are said to be "old before their time." Although his parents were themselves farmers, they made sure to teach him the value of education. They also taught him the love of God, because God had given him to them, and they emphasized the importance of living by the Golden Rule: "Do unto others as you would have them do unto you." They instilled in him the notion that he should be a friend but not get too friendly, and, above all, that he should mind his own business. Lee was content with this lifestyle because, after all, it was the only one he knew.

When he left to attend a black college about three hundred miles from home, his parents gave him fifty dollars and a suitcase packed with bare essentials. He was terrified, but determined to succeed. After an uneventful but successful college experience, he graduated with honors and secured a teaching position in a small town in New Jersey. He saved and sent money home, and he visited as often as he could.

When his father died suddenly, Lee believed he had to return to the farm to help his mother, who was herself elderly and ill. He found a job in a small school district near his parents' homestead and rented out the land for the grazing of cattle and horses. He had no friends in the area and only distant family, but being there for his mother made him feel needed. He also felt that he was, in some way, repaying her for having chosen him as a son.

She was confined to a sickbed for twelve years, during which time Lee refused, despite the advice of her doctor, to put his mother in a nursing home. He took care of her at home, with the help of a nursing assistant during his working hours. When she finally succumbed, Lee experienced a double loss. He became deeply depressed, and, while in counseling, he admitted that he had wanted her to live, despite her failing health, because she was all he had. He finally realized that he didn't know how to live because he didn't know himself, and that he had long held the secret hope that at some point before she died, his mother would tell him about the circumstances surrounding his adoption. He had absolutely no information about his biological family, and this was adding to his grief. Lee believed that he'd had a limited life before his mother's death, but now he had no life at all. He knew how to exist, but he didn't know how to live.

African Americans excel at surviving and existing, but for many, real living, especially after the death of a dependent loved one, can be extremely difficult. These people view death as the end of all life, for they die emotionally with the death of their loved one. Like others who grieve excessively, Lee had to learn that death is a part of life, but that his mother's death was not the end of his life. He had to develop a formula for life without his mother.

My advice to Lee was to put the past in perspective—it was past, period, and what he'd experienced was also past. As to those unanswered questions about his biological family, I asked Lee the following questions: "If you knew, what is it you would know? What difference would it make at this stage of your life?"

A BITTER truth about grieving is that neither tears nor regret nor hostile feelings about the fairness of life will change the present situation. Death is irreversible and will always remain a mystery to those who grieve, but life is for the living and should be lived to the fullest by all.

Learn to express your feelings, but don't expect others to feel what you feel. Seek to restore your spiritual connection with God. Spend time in silent prayer and meditation, asking for strength and faith. Use your experience to assist others in their time of need. Put the past in its proper perspective—it is past, period, and what you experienced is also in the past.

Create a change in your environment, undertake a project, rearrange your personal space. Don't become enslaved to memories, but work at developing new ones. Don't deny yourself the opportunity to love again or trust again, or to explore a different style of living.

Regardless of your loss, love yourself and take care of yourself physically. Don't become dependent on others for your healing, but rather practice self-healing, for healing and happiness begin with you.

Grief is a burden to the griever, and is excessively heavy baggage to carry through life on a daily basis, so learn to unpack that baggage a little at a time. Celebrate the fact that, despite everything you've been through, you are yet alive.

Remind yourself that death is *but* a part of life, and that life consists of other components as well.

In every life there comes a time

To walk in shadows and in sunlight,

To hear silence and song.

To shed tears of sadness and of joy.

To forget what has been taken

And remember

What has been given.

AUTHOR UNKNOWN

✻

LESSONS IN HEALING

- Do not continue to live only as an extension of your deceased loved one. You are an individual who must continue to live until your own life is over.
- Shed your tears, regret your losses, ask God for strength and faith, and then put the past in its proper perspective and live your life to the fullest.
- Express your feelings but don't expect others to feel exactly as you do.

HEALING WORDS

I now seek higher knowledge, as I submit to divine order in all things. I await the ecstasy of a divinely directed life.

❋

THREE

Anger, Fear, and the Loss of Love

Grief brings many different emotions, not all of which are experienced by all people, and not all of which are always understood as manifestations of grief. Among the most common of these feelings is anger at God, the world, or the departed; fear of the unknown future or of death itself; and the loss of a love that can never be regained in quite the same way.

ANGER

> *Anger is only one letter short of danger.*
> ELEANOR ROOSEVELT

Anger is defined in the Random House College Dictionary as "a strong feeling of displeasure and belligerence aroused by a real or supposed wrong." Often the death of a loved one creates a kind of madness in those family members who are left behind, a kind of "raging rage" that must be resolved before the family can cope effectively with the emotional trauma it has collectively experienced.

In the case of the Glover family, their anger was all encompassing. Because "Mom" Glover had always "been there" for all of them—to lend money, to baby-sit, to cook a special meal, or simply to provide words of wisdom—her children and grandchildren seemed to believe that death would pass her by, and she'd be there for them forever.

Few African Americans like to contemplate the death of a vibrant, healthy, but aging loved one, and would prefer to believe, as does a friend of mine when speaking of her eighty-eight-year-old mother, that "She's still going strong, girlfriend! She'll probably outlive me." For the Glovers, however, this inability to imagine life without Mom meant that when she died at a feisty seventy-eight, their collective grief was compounded by shock and expressed as uncontrolled anger.

They were mad at her doctors for not saving her, mad at God for taking her, mad at one another for causing her stress, and mad at Mom for abandoning them. And they were mad at anyone whose mother was still alive and, in their opinion, less worthy than Mom. They found no comfort in either the words or the acts of kindness that were extended to them in their bereavement. All they had were questions: "Why? Why? Why?" and they wanted answers.

It seemed to the Glovers that Mom was too good to die, and they were angry with God, who, as they lamented, did this because he was mean. At this point in their grief-induced anger, many African Americans embrace atheism or agnosticism as a way of getting back at God for causing the death of a loved one. What these people fail to realize, of course, is that by rejecting God, they're rejecting the very source from which they might otherwise have obtained comfort in their time of grief.

What finally brought the Glover family to me for counseling was the realization that by staying mad they were, in fact, destroying their own lives. They were mad on Thanksgiving, mad on Christmas, mad on Mother's Day, on Mom's birthday, and on any other occasion that called for a celebration. And they agreed that their behavior, which they seemed incapable of controlling, would have been "grievous" to Mom.

I realized at once that what they were mourning was losing the sense of security their loved one had provided for each of them individually as well as for the family as a whole. When I asked them at what point they would have been willing to release her to death, they admitted the answer was "never." So I tried to make them understand that death was a part of Mom's life—as it is of all our lives. And I urged them to begin normalizing the grieving process by calling upon all their wonderful memories rather than tainting her memory with the poison of their anger. As they continued in counseling, the Glovers eventually rediscovered not only their spiritual base but also their strong sense of black family pride. As Mom's eldest daughter reminded her siblings, their mother had left them a bountiful inheritance of fine teachings and good examples.

Finally, they agreed that by acting out their feelings of loss, they had failed to honor Mom's memory. And they also came to understand that they were depriving her grandchildren of the celebrations and observances that were part of their family tradition. Christmas and other holidays should have been occasions to recall pleasant memories and find solace in the blessings that had been bestowed upon them, not times to rage at losses beyond their control. I advised them not to try to recreate these occasions "Mom Glover–style," but rather to create new traditions and memories to blend with the old.

At our final session, the whole family came to thank me for guiding them through what they called their darkest hour. We formed a circle, held hands, and, instead of praying,

Mom's children spontaneously began to sing "Precious Memories," a traditional gospel song, which was recorded by Aretha Franklin, James Cleveland, and other gospel artists in the early 1970s.

> Precious memories,
> How they linger,
> How they ever flood my soul,
> In the stillness of the midnight,
> Sacred secrets still unfold.

While we embraced in that moment of joy and sadness, one son remarked, "I've got a feeling everything's gonna be alright." They cried a little and laughed a lot at cherished memories of Mom. And, as a parting gift, I gave them each a bookmark with a verse from David, who, after experiencing deep grief and sorrow, wrote in Psalms 30:5 (KJV):

> For his anger endureth but a moment; in his favor
>   is life.
> Weeping may endure for a night,
> But joy cometh in the morning.

• • •

WHILE THE Glovers' anger was a function of their loving, if unrealistic, belief that Mom was "too good to die," the anger that too often follows the death of a loved one can also result from the survivor's belated perception of some failure or character flaw, real or imagined, on the part of the deceased.

A client who was in therapy for a problem unrelated to death and grieving called to inform me of her husband's sudden demise. Mae was a fragile fifty-six-year-old mother of three adult children, one of whom was mentally limited. Because she did not work—at her husband's insistence—he and he alone had handled all the family finances.

Harvey had been an excellent provider and a good husband and companion (or so Mae thought). After the funeral, she came to my office unannounced and said she simply had to talk with me immediately. Anger (not grief) was etched all over her face, her body was tense, and she was hyperventilating.

Before I could even inquire about the nature of her problem, she began to berate her deceased husband, even wishing that he burn in hell! Between sobs, she said that everything they owned was in his name. As a result, she had no access to any of their bank accounts, which meant she was unable to meet the immediate financial needs of her household. She went on to say that Harvey had never discussed finances with her, and whenever she had tried to bring the subject up, he'd simply assured her that he "would not be dying any time soon," so there was no need to have the discussion.

Now she'd discovered that none of his affairs were in order. She'd been forced to obtain the services of an attorney to establish her husband's estate, when all he'd had to do was to share his knowledge of their personal business and make her joint owner and beneficiary of their assets while he was alive.

Many African American women experience anger after the death of a spouse as a result of behavior very similar to Harvey's. Men of color often demonstrate a desire to control their wives and survivors even from the grave, and they have been known to express anticipatory anger at the very thought that their spouse might remarry and another man enjoy the fruits of their hard labor. I know of one brother who actually said, "Let her new man take care of her after I'm gone."

Mae's children were also angry at their father's poor estate planning, and they were angry and frustrated with Mae for having allowed him to keep her in the dark. Mae, for her part, suddenly felt unloved by her husband of thirty-five years, and her self-esteem immediately evaporated. She was angry with herself for having been so trusting and naïve, and concluded that her married life of unquestioned loyalty and sacrifice had all been in vain.

She had no time to grieve, for every day presented another demand for money. Bills had to be paid, and she had to live somehow. Ironically, she told me, she was old but still too young to collect Harvey's social security check. "How could he do this to me?" she wailed. When her lawyer explained the lengthy process of establishing and distributing his estate, in addition to the estate taxes Mae would have to pay along with his own representation fee, she almost fainted. She talked about Harvey as if he were a dog. She was so angry, she said, she just wanted to spit on his grave. She even expressed regret that she hadn't cremated "his behind," which would have been far less expensive than the lavish laying-out she'd given him. Harvey's insurance policy had provided just enough money to cover the cost of the funeral.

My advice to Mae was to accept things not as they should have or could have been, but as they were in the reality of her present situation. Anger was a luxury she couldn't afford because she needed to focus on her future and the pressing business of survival.

I encouraged her to talk to trusted friends and associates who were widows, both for direction and for emotional support. She later called me to express her total surprise at how many other African American widows had had the same or similar experiences. And she told me about a friend who had lived with a man for twenty-six years although they weren't married. After his death, his estranged wife, whom he'd never divorced, had appeared and laid claim to all he had—and much of what he and Mae's friend had accumulated together.

I advised Mae to "defrost her frozen assets," meaning that she should let her inner strength surface, release her anger, and make a plan for an independent future. She chuck-led when I suggested that she stand on the promise of that song black folks love to sing: "The Lord Will Make a Way Somehow."

I'M HAPPY to report that Mae made it. She sold Harvey's clothes and jewelry, which he'd loved dearly. She sold her mink coat, sold her diamond rings, and got a part-time job to tide her over until the estate was finally settled. She said she's still a little bitter, but she's no longer angry with Harvey, be-cause she now appreciates life on a different level and realizes that any anger she might harbor in her heart against him would only hinder her from going forward. She reminded me of a statement I'd made at a group therapy session about dealing with anger. The statement was a simple one, but, she said, it had a lasting impact on her. The words I'd addressed to this group of angry and bitter clients were, "You can't think crooked and walk straight." Look ahead to a new beginning. File failure and disappointment in a mental box and never open it again.

SADLY, FOR our people, there is a devastating and self-destructive form of anger experienced by survivors that is, too often, the result of what they consider the inadequate health care received by the deceased.

In its June 1999 issue, the *National Vital Statistics Reports* listed the top ten causes of death among African Americans as heart disease, cancer, stroke, AIDS, auto accidents, homicide, diabetes, flu/pneumonia, lung disease, and birth defects. The same report also indicated that we have a higher percentage of chronic diseases and die from them more frequently than other populations. In addition, the U.S. Department of Health and Human Services, along with the American Medical Association, have acknowledged that there is a disparity between the quality of health care received by blacks and that given to other ethnic groups. An alarming number of African Americans have inadequate or no health insurance and, as a result, receive inferior care. According to the most recent statistics released by the Department of Health and Human Services, black children under the age of thirteen die of AIDS at a rate nine times greater than whites, while we succumb to hypertension four times more frequently than whites. And there can be no doubt that when death is perceived to be caused by second-class medical treatment, the grief experienced by surviving loved ones becomes that much more difficult and complicated to process.

I remember in particular a client who came to me expressing her bitter hatred for all whites because of the poor medical care given her sister, who had died of a brain tumor. Pam was so consumed by anger that her obsession was affecting her own health. Her sister, she said, had been complaining of constant headaches and dizziness, but when she went to the doctor she'd simply been told to slow down, take over-the-counter pain medication twice daily, and watch her diet. When the condition didn't improve after several months, she returned to the doctor, who this time concluded that the problem was probably a sinus condition. Finally, the pain became so intense that Pam had taken her sister to the emergency room, where X rays finally showed the tumor. Pam blamed both her sister's doctor and her health insurance, which didn't cover extensive testing, for the fact that the tumor wasn't discovered sooner, when it might have been operable. And, like many African Americans, she believed that the health care given blacks by white health professionals and hospitals was not equal to that received by whites.

In the same counseling group was also Theo, a sixty-three-year-old man who had recently retired from government employment with the expectation that he and his wife would enjoy their remaining years together. Sadly, his wife's lung cancer had been misdiagnosed, and for months she'd been treated for an allergy with antibiotics and cough syrup. As in the case of Pam's sister, her disease wasn't discovered until she was taken to the hospital on an emergency basis, when it was too late for treatment to be effective.

Theo, too, was filled with hatred for all white people, and much of my counseling was devoted to trying to make both him and Pam understand that such negative emotions would only prevent their healthy grieving and that they would somehow have to give up their hatred if they were ever to enjoy the solace that comes from loving memories of the departed. By the time I met them, Pam had lost a tremendous amount of weight and wasn't sleeping well, Theo was drinking more than he should, and both of them were in danger of allowing their own health to deteriorate as a result of their inability to let go of their anger. I urged them as strongly as I could to try to "get past the past" so that they would be able to heal and move on, as we all must.

Although their feelings about the quality of care given to their loved ones was not necessarily without reason, both Pam and Theo, along with other African Americans, needed to be reminded that there are both good and bad people of all races, including our own, and that we should never allow our experience with a particular individual to color our feelings about any group as a whole. And, above all, we must never allow our own pain and suffering to become a form of emotional connection to our loved one.

FEAR

> *For the thing which I greatly feared is come*
> *upon me, and that which I was afraid of is*
> *come unto me . . .*

JOB 3:25

For some, fear can be so overwhelming that they allow it to control their life. For example, people fear dying in a plane crash, so they refuse to fly. After all, they say by way of justification, "If God had wanted man to fly, He would have given

him wings." Others fear death on the highway, so they limit
vehicular travel. In much the same way, many people are just
plain afraid of dying and are scared (to death) of dead people, even their own loved ones.

There's an old African American saying that goes "Everybody wants to go to Heaven, but nobody wants to die,"
and another whispered saying, especially among black senior
citizens, is "I *know* that heaven is my home, but I'm not home-
sick." For many people, these statements express a fear of
death and dying in spite of their firm belief in heaven as their
eternal home. While death is life's one certainty, many continue to fear it, even by association.

Kia, a client who was in therapy for thanatophobia (fear
of death), was afraid of anything death-related. She was so
afraid of dead people that, at the age of forty-three, she had
never attended a funeral or viewed a dead body. When her
own mother died, she was in a state of panic because before
she could grieve she would have to confront her fear. For the
first time in her life, she was experiencing not only fear, but
also guilt and embarrassment as the result of her phobia.

Kia was distraught, and my counseling would have to be
on a very fast track—she was responsible for coordinating
her mother's funeral arrangements. She felt totally incapable

of performing this task and was at a loss as to how to handle the situation. And because both she and her mother suffered from diabetes and high blood pressure, she was further fearful that her own death was just a matter of time. The funeral, meanwhile, was on hold. Kia's family was too frustrated with the situation, and too angry with her, to provide the understanding or express the sympathy she needed. Her relatives simply thought she was being both stupid and foolish. "The dead can't hurt you," people told her. "They can make you hurt yourself," she replied. Her fear of death took precedence even over grieving the loss of her mother, whom she had loved dearly in life.

Kia quieted her own feelings of guilt by saying, "Momma knew how scared I was of dead people and the thought of death." I learned in counseling that her fear had been created, at least in part, by deeply instilled superstitions. She recalled stories she'd heard in childhood about dead people who, although cold and lifeless, nevertheless made noises, often returning to communicate with the living. She also believed that death was contagious within a family. There's a saying, handed down among blacks from one generation to the next, that death "comes in threes" within a family or a circle of friends. Kia began to wonder if she were the next in line, and she wanted to avoid all contact with death at any level, which included making any decisions about her mother's funeral arrangements.

People who suffer from thanatophobia need to seek counseling *before* they're confronted with death on a personal level. The griever's fear of death can cause feelings of dread, anxiety, fright, alarm, terror, and panic, as well as physical illness. The counselor needs to identify and explore the specific sources of the client's fear. Kia developed symptoms including loss of appetite, rapid heartbeat, severe headaches, insomnia, dizzy spells, numbness, and panic attacks. Although she was advised by friends and family to seek immediate medical attention for these ailments, there is no medicine that can cure the emotional illness Kia, and others like her, experience.

Slowly, spiritual therapy is finding its way into the African American community. This kind of therapy addresses the core of the sufferer's fear by seeking to open the windows of his very soul and encouraging spiritual growth. One important aspect of this therapy is to help the victim establish some degree of tolerance for death without being traumatized by it. African Americans have always practiced religion and have adhered to long-held rituals, yet not many have sought to develop the understanding of life and death that comes with spiritual growth. Spiritual growth minimizes fear of death by identifying dying as a transitory crossing over into a spiritual realm.

For generations, African Americans viewed God as a man with unchallenged powers, who "sees all you do and hears all you say." He was portrayed on the backs of fans in black churches as having a long blond beard, alluring blue eyes, a faint smile, and outstretched hands. After the "black power" movement of the 1960s, this visual image was modi fied, and God was shown as a nappyheaded, thicklipped be ing of African descent. But neither of these images presents an accurate picture of the Creator, for God is *spirit*—the spirit of love, joy, peace, and mercy. First John, 4:18 (KJV) says, "Perfect love casteth out fear." Perfected love is not phys ical but spiritual, and when one is able to experience this kind of love, one no longer has any reason to fear hurt or harm from the dead.

In addition, if one has experienced this kind of mean ingful love in an earthly relationship, whether with family, a friend, or an associate, one would be insulting the deceased's memory to think that person would harm one in any way, be cause love extends beyond death.

Ultimately, Kia did what she had to do; she made it through the funeral. Although she is still somewhat fearful of death, she fears no evil and is now maturing spiritually at a moderate pace.

FEAR OF death itself is, however, only one way this crippling emotion is likely to manifest. Fear of living is another. It's understandable that anyone long accustomed to following life's path in the company of a loving companion would fear sudden abandonment on the trail with no clear markers to follow. For many African Americans, this kind of fear can be overwhelming.

That's exactly what happened to Norma when her husband, Mitch, died. She was "scared to death" of facing life without her soul mate, and she was truly afraid she wouldn't make it. Finally, she was introduced to me by a caring sister-in-law who had previously received counseling for a stress-related problem and been pleased with the results.

Norma was uncomfortable on her first visit, and her all-encompassing fear was patently obvious. She was afraid of being in my office and more afraid of her reason for being there. It was important for her to make me understand that she was "afraid" but not "crazy." I asked her to be more specific about her fears, and the bottom line was that she feared everything! I asked her to focus on whether her fear was of life or of death. In her terror, however, she took this as a trick question and was afraid of giving the wrong answer!

I noticed that in appearance and demeanor she was like many African American women who even in adulthood retain many childish characteristics. She was a little pudgy, cute but not pretty, and she spoke in a high-pitched voice. At the age of forty-eight, she still wore her hair in a ponytail with bangs on her forehead.

When I suggested that she simply begin by telling me something about her life history, she relaxed a little and explained that she was the youngest of four children and the only girl in a fun-loving, wonderful family. She'd been spoiled by her parents and adored by her protective older brothers. She'd been attracted to Mitch, she said, because, like her father and brothers, he treated her "like a queen."

They were married when Norma was twenty-two, and Mitch, at twenty-six, was already a hardworking, settled, and mature young man. They'd decided against having children, and Norma delighted in being babied and pampered throughout her twenty-six years of blissful marriage. Mitch helped with the household chores and enjoyed going with her to the mall and helping to select her clothes. Norma had never worked outside the home or learned to drive a car because Mitch took care of her and took her wherever she wanted to go. "We had a beautiful marriage" is how she described their relationship.

On occasion, Mitch would go fishing with his buddies, and Norma sometimes spent weekends with her family, but they'd seldom been separated for any extended period of time. After Mitch's death, Norma was mourning that separation, but she was also fearful of being without his companionship, protection, and guidance. She told me that someone from her family or his had been with her every night since his death, because they knew how afraid she was of being alone. Now, three months later, Norma was aware that this arrangement wouldn't last forever. She needed to confront her fears and establish a life without Mitch, and she was afraid of starting this new journey.

Many African Americans whose lives, like Norma's, have been blessed with the comfort and protection of a loving and wholesome relationship are petrified by the changes that are automatically mandated in their life by the death of that companion. I advised Norma to consider the vast difference between being alone and being lonely, helping her to understand that her greatest fear was of loneliness. It's not a secret, I told her, that we all have an appointment with death in our future, but our most immediate and pressing appointment is with life, right now! She shuddered when I reminded her that the relatives in her life who had been serving as Mitch's temporary substitutes would eventually, one day, die too. But I also counseled her to realize that they were there for her now and that she was not alone in coping with her grief and fear.

At last, we were able to work through Norma's feelings of insecurity and helplessness so that she could move on with a more realistic attitude and approach to her future. While I almost always recommend that a griever return to his or her spiritual base in our Christian faith, I also caution mourners not to use religion as a crutch, but rather to see it as a guiding comfort and source of strength during trying times. Norma found such strength in Mitch's memory as well as in her re-established faith in God. And she found additional strength in the fellowship of others who were striving for the faith.

Whenever she was faced with a decision, she would first pray, then she would think, "What would Mitch do?" in this situation. By the end of our counseling sessions, she had decided to sell the house they'd shared and move into an apartment. She bought new furniture, and she learned to drive. These were major undertakings, and Norma was pleased with her accomplishments. She changed her hairstyle, lost some weight, and declared, "I've grown up now, and I know Mitch would be proud."

LOSS OF LOVE

"I've lost that loving feeling!"

African Americans have always expressed their feelings of and thoughts about love through music. The lyrics of black songs, sung by soulful black artists in every genre from jazz to blues to rock and roll to gospel, have had as their inspiration...love. "If lovin' you is wrong, I don't wanna do right; Always and forever, I'll love only you; Our love is here to stay; For your love, I would do anything, I would go anywhere, for your love." These are just a few of the musical sentiments expressed in these songs. Blacks are, without doubt, people who love loving and who are known for doing almost everything in the name of love. Ask any African American adult over the age of forty how many "whippings" he (or she) received as a child "because I love you" (notwithstanding the fact that such a love-inspired beating would now be considered child abuse). Blacks *love* to eat, *love* to cook, *love* to party, and are passionate in their love for family and friends. Blacks also *love* heroes and bless their celebrities with unconditional love, whatever act or deed they may commit.

The grief that accompanies loss of love is complex because its direct impact upon the griever is so great. The core of this grief is centered on the relationship that existed between the deceased and the survivor. Not only does the survivor miss the feeling of being loved, but he or she often feels that he cannot or will not ever love, or be loved in that way again. Some "good-loving" African Americans in the 1950s, who enjoyed experiencing sexual satisfaction in the name of love, described love as "a feeling when you feel it, and you don't know what you're feeling when you feel it." When they lose that feeling, people often experience an accompanying sense of being abandoned. "A lonely loss" is how one client, named Chey, described her emotional state to me. "A loss of companionship," she cried, "because we did everything together."

Chey came into counseling confused about her feelings over the loss of the love of her life. She was "lost without him," she said, and feeling disconnected from life. She felt that when Kenny died a part of her died with him.

Eventually, she came to realize that she was grieving both for her loss of Kenny and for what she viewed as her duty to him. She had loved doing things for him and missed being needed by him. She felt that the longer she mourned and grieved openly, the greater was her testimony to their unique love. As a result, she wore black for an entire year because she believed that this outward display of continuing grief represented an unbroken bond between them. Before she was able to loosen this bond and readjust to life without Kenny's special love, Chey had to process a gradual release of each detail of their relationship.

The lesson she and others need to learn is that although it is therapeutic to remember and review the love we shared with another, we cannot relive it. Rather than wallow in our fear of letting go of that love, we should celebrate the joy of having experienced loving and being loved to the fullest extent.

MEMORIES

A limb has fallen from the tree,
I keep hearing a voice say, "Grieve not for me."
Remember the best times, the laughter, the songs,
The good life I lived while God made me strong.
Continue my heritage, I'm counting on you.
Keep smiling and surely the sun will shine through.

My mind is at ease, my soul is at rest
Remembering Oh! How I was truly blessed.
Continue traditions, no matter how small.
Go on with life, don't just stare at the wall.
I miss you so dearly, so keep up your chin
Until the day comes, we are together again.

AUTHOR UNKNOWN

THIS KIND of grief is not, however, always related to the death of a lover or a spouse. Brenda, the youngest of three daughters and one son in a close-knit African American family, experienced just such a loss with the sudden death of her loving father when she was just thirteen years old. At the funeral, Brenda was "out of control" and the center of attention. For years afterward, she exhibited a pattern of problem behavior, and whenever her family or friends tried to motivate her to change her ways and get on with her life, she rebelled even more.

When she finally came to me for counseling, it was simply to avoid being declared a total "mental case." She ranted and raved that no one understood how she felt about her father's death. She'd been "Daddy's little girl," and when he died, her status died as well. Brenda no longer felt special. She'd "lost that loving feeling," and she grieved her father's physical absence from her life.

It was challenging for me to help Brenda understand the true meaning of the word "loss." To lose something doesn't mean the end of its existence; it simply means that what you've lost is no longer available for you. And so it is with the loss of a loved one. Love doesn't die with the loss of the person; it remains in your memory, and your life should be a celebration of that special love.

I advised Brenda to honor her father's love for her by helping that love to grow, even in spirit, because, had he lived, his love for her would certainly have matured to another level. He would have continued to love her unconditionally through the various stages of her growth and development. And I couldn't help sharing with her the words written by Elizabeth Barrett Browning who, when facing death, wrote to her husband, Robert Browning, "I shall but love thee even better after death."

LIKE BRENDA and Norma, many African Americans feel totally bereft when faced with the loss of what they consider a special kind of love. What these people need to remember in order to get through the grieving process and move on is that anyone who loved them so completely would also want them to be happy and to continue to grow and mature. By turning their back on life, they fail to honor the memory of their loved one by failing to live up to his or her expectations for them.

LESSONS IN HEALING

- Never allow your wonderful memories to be tainted by the poison of your anger.
- Learn to accept things as they are, not as they could or should have been.
- Give up the negative emotions that prevent healthy grieving.
- Don't allow your own pain and suffering to become your only connection with your loved one.
- Let go of the fear of letting go and celebrate the joy of having been loved to the fullest.

HEALING WORDS

There are times that I experience a "rock bottom" feeling. A feeling of depression and fear simply overwhelms me without warning. I now know that when this occurs, I will aim for the top of the rock!

FOUR

*

Guilt and Self-Forgiveness

Don't Play the Blame Game!

Down through the years, fire and brimstone preachers have told African Americans that, according to scripture, "you reap what you sow" (Gal. 6:7). And for some black folks that means "what goes around comes around." As a result, many of us look upon the death of a loved one as a kind of divine retribution for our own past sins, unkind deeds, or less than exemplary behavior.

Such was the case for my client, Miriam, a thirty-three-year-old paralegal. In her early teens, Miriam had become pregnant after a brief sexual relationship with her then-boyfriend. Knowing that her mother would "kill" her if she found out, and realizing that neither she nor her boyfriend was ready for the responsibility of parenthood, Miriam decided to have an abortion. She didn't regret her decision, but it became her lifelong secret.

The intervening years were good to Miriam. She had a well-paying job, a nice apartment, and she had developed a meaningful relationship with a supportive and loving African American man. They were both ecstatic when Miriam gave birth to a beautiful daughter, whom they named Joi because she was the joy of Miriam's life.

When the baby developed a series of infections and illnesses and finally died at the age of three, Miriam immediately concluded that Joi's death was her punishment for having had an abortion. She was overwhelmed by guilt and went into a deep depression. Her mate had to virtually drag her to a counseling session, where her pain and anguish were almost palpable. Rocking back and forth, she mumbled softly, "It's all my fault, God is punishing me. Oh, God, I want my baby, please forgive me." For the first time in her life, Miriam then told the story of her past sexual activity and her teenage abortion. She felt somewhat purged, but she was still convinced that there was no explanation for Joi's death other than divine retribution.

Eventually, she came to understand that spiritual and self-forgiveness are companions in overcoming guilt and that both are necessary for overcoming grief. Not only must we forgive ourselves for past mistakes, but we must also obtain inner peace by understanding that our Creator is not a vindictive spirit and forgives us even when we do not forgive ourselves.

THERE IS, however, another kind of guilt that can result either from a sense of *not* having done everything one could while our loved one was alive—in other words guilt by omission—or from the feeling that we committed an act that contributed to the death—guilt by commission. And the griever's own sense of guilt can be compounded by the opinions of others who sit in judgment—silent or otherwise—of the circumstances surrounding a particular death.

This kind of guilt, while related to simple regret, is different because it usually results from some specific act related directly to the death rather than from the mourner's ongoing relationship with the deceased. In many instances, for example, a family member must make a decision about a medical procedure such as surgery, an amputation, or a radical treatment that may or may not prolong the life of the patient. If death results from that decision, the griever then goes through a period of darkness and despair, wondering whether his loved one would have lived if he or she had made a different choice.

Such intense and extreme feelings of guilt manifest themselves in various ways, depending on the manner of death and the options that were or were not chosen by the survivor. Self-punishment, low self-esteem, severe depression, and addictive behaviors are all signs of guilty grieving. Some who grieve in this way feel unworthy of any future happiness and will actually prevent good things from happening to them.

Such was the case for Marissa, who had done nothing but cry and feel guilty for nine months before she came to me for counseling at the suggestion of a co-worker. Her mother, Val, had suffered cardiac arrest and died during an operation for lung cancer. Val had resisted the surgery, applying the old black philosophy, "If it ain't botherin' me, why should I bother it?" Marissa, who had pressured her mother to have the operation, was now devastated and feeling totally responsible for her death.

During our first session, she told me her father had abandoned the family when she was just six years old and vanished from their lives. Val had worked hard to provide

Marissa with a good Catholic school education. Marissa had excelled in school and been awarded a full scholarship to the state university. Upon graduation, she'd landed a good position with a Fortune 500 company where she'd received several promotions, so that now, at the age of thirty-two, her annual salary was in excess of $100,000 a year.

Marissa had insisted that her mother retire from her job as a state employee at the age of fifty-four, and had vowed to take care of her as long as she lived. She took her mother on a yearly cruise and spoiled her with luxury items and a comfortable lifestyle. In effect, she had assumed the role of mother to her mother. She made sure Val had regular medical and dental checkups, paid her monthly bills, and made all the major decisions in her life. Val, for her part, had enjoyed being spoiled by her loving and grateful daughter. Now Marissa rebuked herself constantly for insisting on the surgery and was convinced her mother would have lived longer if only she'd not had the operation.

Other family members believed that Val's cardiac arrest had been caused by her fear of the procedure and blamed Marissa for "making her go through with it." This, of course, only reinforced Marissa's guilt feelings, and as a result, she had become a virtual recluse. She felt she didn't deserve to have a social life or to pursue personal happiness of any kind. Marissa was her own sentencing judge, and she had sentenced herself to a life without joy.

Because of her grief, she felt the need to communicate her sorrow to her mother's spirit. To absolve grievers of their guilt, some companies are now offering caskets with little drawers in which the griever can put a note of love and apology or other mementos of his or her bond with the deceased. Marissa had bought one of these caskets and had placed in the drawer a lengthy letter expressing her deep sorrow and asking her mother's forgiveness. Like many African Americans, she had hoped to have a dream or receive some kind of sign that her mother didn't hold her decision against her. Now she was hurt and disappointed because she didn't feel forgiven.

As a counselor, I believe it's important for those who are grieving to be gradually reintroduced to some form of humor. Often those people who attempt to support the griever are uncomfortable laughing or joking in his or her presence, and some who grieve go for extended periods without any respite from their mourning. So I took the risk of sharing with Marissa a little mortician-trade humor. The story goes that one family who, like Marissa, had selected a casket with a memory drawer, placed a substantial sum of money in the drawer because the deceased had often expressed his fear of dying broke and had always carried a "stash of cash" in his pocket. When the family left the funeral home, the mortician removed the money and replaced it with his personal check, along with a note advising the deceased that the check was good, and he should feel free to cash it whenever he arrived at his final destination!

Marissa began to smile, then laugh, and, oh, how she laughed! She laughed until she began to cry. And through her tears, she laughed at herself for forgetting to put her mother's reading glasses in the drawer with the note. "No wonder I haven't heard from her; she can't read without her glasses!" I still rejoice at this gratifying breakthrough brought on by the power of laughter.

Marissa made rapid progress in counseling once she was able to see that her mother's death had been beyond her control and that, although Val had not been in pain, her lung condition would probably have resulted in a long illness, which neither of them had wanted.

I counseled her to feel good about the close relationship she and Val had shared and to reflect on the life her mother had enjoyed because of her generosity, affection, and gratitude. Slowly she came to understand that her mother would have wanted her to be happy and that she would be honoring

Val's memory by regaining her vivacious personality and getting back to the business of living her life to the fullest.

Marissa felt she could end her counseling sessions when, as she told me, for the first time since her mother's death, she'd had a beautiful dream about her. "She looked so happy, and she smiled at me in the dream." Marissa was at last free of guilt, and she said, "I feel good!"

IT'S IMPORTANT for African Americans who feel guilty about the death of a loved one not to mask their guilt with excessive drinking, drug use, or overindulgence of any kind. Rather, the griever must learn to face his guilt and strive to overcome self-abuse and unwarranted self-punishment. The Creator is a forgiving and understanding god. One of the attributes I love about God is His willingness to look beyond our faults and meet our every need.

Learn that just as we are given the gift of life one day at a time, so are we forgiven on a daily basis. Our guilt will vanish only if we acknowledge our frail mortality and express regret for our mistakes. While we can't rewind the tape of life, we can fast-forward to doing good for others, reaping the harvest of positive seeds and good deeds sowed in another person's life.

• • •

THE INABILITY to forgive oneself frequently results in chronic and sometimes excessive grieving that can extend over a long period of time. Confronting the challenge to forgive oneself is both an isolating and isolated phase of bereavement. Many who feel guilty because of their perceived contribution to the death of a loved one are at a loss to know how to forgive themselves.

One client came into counseling desperately seeking a way to overcome her guilt about the accidental death of her cousin. "I can never forgive myself for what happened," Juanita told me. She and Thelma had always been more like sisters, she said, and as adults the bond between them had grown even stronger. They shopped together, took vacations together, and talked on the phone for hours. Juanita was forty-six years old when we met, a social worker who was divorced with no children. Thelma, who had never married, was fifty years old at the time of her death. She was an elementary school teacher who loved her job, Juanita recalled with a tearful smile. She had brought to the session a photo album full of photos of the "golden girls"—vacationing in Nassau, celebrating their having hit the thousand-dollar jackpot in Las Vegas, toasting the new year with champagne.

These two had genuinely enjoyed the things they did together and were grateful for the freedom and financial resources to do as they pleased.

The tragedy occurred when Thelma accompanied Juanita to a social worker's conference in Detroit, and they decided to extend their trip by spending a few days in Canada after the meeting. Juanita recalled that the trip had been special, and they'd both had a ball. Thelma had just purchased a new Lexus SUV, and they were both anxious to put it on the road.

Thelma started the twelve-hour drive home and drove for five hours while Juanita napped. When they stopped for gas, Thelma said she was tired and Juanita took over the wheel. She recalls driving cautiously, but for some reason she lost control of the car and veered off the highway. The Lexus tumbled down an embankment and turned over three times. When the police and paramedics arrived, Thelma was pronounced dead at the scene with a broken neck. Juanita had miraculously escaped with only minor facial scratches and a broken arm.

When she arrived at the hospital, Juanita was in shock and a state of total disbelief. She immediately sank into a morass of multilevel grief, experiencing not only shock and disbelief, but also anger, severe depression, fear, and guilt.

Because the accident had occurred several hundred miles from home, she was alone and frightened, and she found the police questioning humiliating and offensive. Had she been drinking? Did she use drugs? Had she and Thelma argued about something that might have upset her and caused her to lose control of the car? "No, no, no!" she recalled screaming. To complicate matters, all her identification had been in her purse, in the car, which had burned completely. She was without insurance documents and was too upset and confused to think about whom she should call at home. All she knew was that she wanted to see Thelma.

After being treated and questioned, Juanita had to identify Thelma's body. One can only imagine how traumatic that must have been. As she was telling me the story, Juanita began to relive the incident all over again. She cried and screamed as she recalled crying and screaming when she saw her cousin's body in the hospital morgue. She remembered wanting to hold Thelma and tell her she was sorry, so sorry, for causing the accident.

Eventually, Juanita's brother, Lance, received a call from a hospital nurse who informed him what had happened. He arrived several hours later to take his sister home, a trip that was still a blur in her memory. Lance asked questions about the accident, and when he began to talk about bringing

Thelma's body home for burial, Juanita says she lost it. Lance was afraid she was having a nervous breakdown on the spot. When they finally arrived home, she was bombarded with more questions than sympathy from friends and family, which only added to her grief and despair. When I met her, she was still bitter about that.

AFRICAN AMERICANS are famous for wanting to know all the nitty-gritty death details, such as "What happened?" "What did he die of?" Or, as in Thelma's case, "How did it happen?" We can be virtually relentless in our quest for the low-down, but we must realize that, especially in cases of dramatic death such as Thelma's, it's extremely insensitive for us to expect the survivor to tell her story over and over just to satisfy our inquiring minds. Juanita told me of comments people had made about her possibly driving too fast or not being as alert as she should have been.

She admitted she felt guilty for having survived and now wished she'd died along with her cousin. "It's my fault she's dead," she said again and again when discussing her feelings. She'd begun to believe she'd done something to cause the accident: Had the Tylenol she'd taken made her drowsy? Had she taken her hand off the wheel to reach for a cigarette?

Had she not noticed a curve in the road? She didn't realize that by constantly focusing on the accident, she was always in a state of re-grieving, which kept Thelma alive in her mind.

Juanita confessed that she'd always assumed her close friendship with her cousin would last forever. She and Thelma had jokingly talked about living out their old age together in an old folks home and laughing about how "they were hell when they were well." Now she had to change her assumptions about her future.

MANY AFRICAN Americans find security in a never-changing existence. They adapt to the familiar way of life, whether that life is good or bad. Just ask some blacks "How're things going?" and they'll respond "Same-o, same-o," meaning nothing is changed and "I can deal with that."

Juanita, like others, was comfortable thinking she knew what tomorrow would bring. She found it difficult to adjust to living beyond her comfort zone, with an unknown agenda for the future. She was surprised when I told her she would probably always experience some feelings of guilt, but that she shouldn't permit her guilt to destroy her. I advised her to admit the possibility of some responsibility for the accident and see it as just that—a tragic accident, not a deliberate act

on her part. I advised Juanita to begin to think of an appropriate way to atone for Thelma's death. This wasn't easy for
her, but she understood it was vital for her grief recovery.

She also needed to renew her spiritual connection with
God. She'd stopped praying and going to church because of
her anger and her guilt. And she still didn't understand why
her life had been spared.

The purpose of grief counseling is not to provide answers to unanswerable questions, but to assist the griever in
coping with loss and adjusting to life without his or her loved
one. Juanita had to realize that life does go on, and that, in
order to live her life with any degree of sanity, she'd have to
find a way to feel forgiven and grieve in the normal manner.

Juanita's guilt was compounded by the fact that she was
Thelma's sole beneficiary, and she felt unworthy of such generosity. I suggested that she memorialize her cousin by establishing a scholarship in Thelma's name at her alma mater.
I also urged her to review her image of herself and begin to
appreciate the things about her that Thelma had loved.

Gradually Juanita was emancipated from the bondage of
her self-imposed condemnation, until she was once more able
to see herself as "a good person who would not knowingly
hurt anybody," and to believe Thelma knew that as well. Although Juanita made progress in therapy, she found that her

gain was not without pain. As she began to forgive herself, she also began to experience the pain of lost friendship and to miss the social activities she'd shared with Thelma.

An important life lesson is that we shouldn't depend on others for our happiness, because true happiness comes from within; the joy we share with others only enhances that which is already inside us. After thirty-nine counseling sessions, Juanita realized it was time to begin again. "Yes, life is full of new beginnings," I told her as we hugged good-bye, and I gave her a copy of the words to a sacred song by R. C. Ward, a noted hymnologist of the 1800s, who wrote:

> When waves of affliction sweep over the soul,
> And sunlight is hidden from view,
> If ever you're tempted to fret or complain,
> Just think of His goodness to you.
> When dear ones are taken away from you here,
> You loved with affection so true,
> Look unto the Savior for strength to endure,
> And think of His goodness to you.

ABOUT A year after our final session, Juanita called me to re-port that she'd met a wonderful widower, and they had developed a beautiful friendship. She was enjoying the attention and affection he bestowed on her, and she lovingly accused Thelma of plotting their meeting from heaven. She viewed this new friendship not as a replacement for what she'd shared with Thelma but as a message from her cousin that said, "Be happy and know that God loves you, and so do I."

✺

LESSONS IN HEALING

- Remember that our Creator is an understanding and forgiving God and forgive yourself for past transgressions real or imagined.
- Remember that your loved one would want you to be happy.
- Remember that God helps those who help themselves and don't be ashamed or afraid to seek the help that is now available to us from trained grief counselors, ministers, and support groups.
- Always remember to laugh; humor can be a great healer.

HEALING WORDS

Today I realize that being in touch and in tune with the will of the Almighty for my life should be first at all times! This and only this will give me the power and the strength to strive and survive.

FIVE

Grieving Before Death

Why is life so tragic?

Many families, especially when someone is terminally ill, have advance notice of impending death. In such instances, loved ones are given the chance to spend time with one another, share emotions, and heal past misunderstandings. There is also time for loved ones to set priorities and for the patient to get his or her affairs in order.

During this time, the patient may be spoiled, coddled, and showered with attention. It's important, however, that family and friends not deny the dying an opportunity to discuss his or her concerns, fears, and other feelings. Too often, when the sick attempt to voice these fears and feelings, they are hushed with well-meaning comments like "Hold on, have faith," or are given false hope of recovery. In this way, they are actually denied the opportunity to grieve for their own death while they are still alive.

Anticipatory grief is the time of grieving prior to the actual death. While having advance notice of an impending death affords friends and families the opportunity for pre-death bereavement, it can also be a time of awkwardness and anxiety. Family members and close friends may disagree about what to tell the terminally ill or those who inquire about the patient's condition. How do you say "he's dying"? Many black folks would hasten to protest, "Don't say that! God is capable of all things," denying reality and holding out hope to the very end.

Until recently, many terminally ill African Americans were taken home to die once there was nothing more to be done for them medically and, as the saying went, "it was just a matter of time." From that point on, family members tended to arrange their lives around the impending death, rather than the life, of the soon-to-be-departed. Pre-death mourning meant no loud noises, no laughing, keeping the sick room in darkness, and speaking in hushed tones. It was considered dishonorable to discuss death in the presence of the dying. "Don't talk about it; you're going to be alright," the patient would be falsely and foolishly assured.

I had a personal encounter with just such a situation several years ago, when my dear friend Jeffrey was ill with terminal cancer. He knew he was dying and wanted to put his affairs in order, but his friends and family kept telling him not to think about it and just to concentrate on getting well. We knew he was dying, but we didn't want *him* to know we'd given up hope of a miracle. To this day, I regret being one of those who thwarted his desire to articulate his last wishes. Only after his death did we learn that his estate was in disarray, and we were stunned to discover that he had been extremely wealthy.

Afterward, we who had been close to him grieved because we'd denied Jeffrey the opportunity to grieve for us. Dying patients need to be allowed to express their sorrow at leaving their loved ones, and those who will survive need to express the grief of their anticipated loss.

ROLAND, a client of mine, was literally forced into therapy by his family during his wife's thirteen-month illness. She had suffered a massive stroke that left her severely brain-damaged and immobile. Roland wanted to oversee and manage her care personally. He refused to accept the fact that it would be better to let her die rather than to continue to keep her alive in a vegetative state. In fact, he stated emphatically that he didn't care what shape she was in; he just wanted her to live. He didn't need her to respond to anything. If she just lay there he'd be satisfied. Although other family members, some of whom had distanced themselves emotionally from the situation, were already grieving her death, Roland refused even to consider disconnecting her from life support. Rather, he hated them for not having a positive attitude about her possible recovery.

In therapy, I encouraged Roland to discuss what he imag-ined his life would be without his wife. He admitted that he was afraid of the responsibility for making decisions con-cerning their small children, and he was fearful of ending up the same way as his wife. We discussed at length the ways his wife's prolonged dying was causing him to neglect his chil-dren and preventing him from providing them with the se-curity and stability she would have wanted them to have. He confessed that whenever he wasn't actually at the hospital, he would panic each time someone came to the door or the tele-phone rang.

The more we talked, the more it became apparent that Roland was experiencing profound guilt about making what he now considered to have been unreasonable demands upon his wife: that she acquiesce to his choice of vacations and out-ings; that he had not allowed her to go to a casino, which was something she'd longed to experience; that he had never allowed her a night out on her own without the children. It was painful for him to discuss the regret he was now feeling for his chauvinistic attitude, and he wanted his wife to live so that he could make up for his past behavior.

Like many people, he was finding it difficult to accept the finality of his wife's impending death. And, also like many, he was going into multiple stages of deep grief all at once. It's not uncommon, upon learning of a terminal illness, for a maelstrom of thoughts to swirl through the minds of the patient's loved ones: "How did this happen?" "Why?" and, of course, "When will death actually occur?"

Roland was overwhelmed by shock. How could it really be *his* wife whose life was rapidly coming to an end? He was angry with the unknown god who was in total control of the deadly situation. He was afraid of facing the future without her, and he was fearful of the responsibility her death would place upon him. In addition, Roland didn't know how to release his wife and accept the reality of her untimely death.

In counseling, he resisted forgiving himself; he felt better feeling bad. Roland reveled in self-punishment, and he felt unworthy of divine forgiveness—if, he said, such a thing existed. "I was so wrong about so many things; I should be the one dying, not her," he whispered in a soft voice.

Many African Americans lose a degree of self-esteem during their first encounter with pre-grieving because their entire existence has revolved around their loved one. One bitter truth is that people often confuse their dependency on the dying person with love. Roland unquestionably loved his wife, but his *need* for her exceeded his love.

It's interesting if unfortunate that, for many, pre-death grief involves selfishness, because the griever's thoughts are focused on his own life after the death of the loved one. "How am I going to make it? I can't handle this! What am I going to do? My life is over, too. Who will be there for *me*? I'm scared." The needs and concerns of "me" and "I" take precedence over concern for the dying, which indicates a fear of life, not really of death.

I advised Roland to invoke self-forgiveness by acknowledging that he'd made mistakes or could have acted differently in his marriage. His challenge was to change his mind-set regarding his role as an African American male and to adjust his domineering and controlling nature. That adjustment was important to make not only for himself, but also for the sake of a healthy and happy relationship with his children. I also encouraged Roland to talk with his wife, even in her comatose state, to express his sorrow and reassure her of his love and gratitude for the role she'd played in his life. I pointed out to him that many people believe that a sincere message from the heart is received in the heart and spirit of the person who is dying, even if he or she is beyond conscious understanding.

Although dreading the anticipated loss, Roland, like others in his situation, had to graduate from dread in order to release his soon-to-be-departed loved one. The one who is dying is, after all, the one who is actually experiencing the actual pain and discomfort. And there can be no doubt that, in many instances, the patient is prepared to be released from ongoing suffering when all hope of a recovery has passed.

In Roland's counseling group there was a young, well-educated thirty-three-year-old widow named Venus whose thirty-seven-year-old husband, Mark, had died after a six-month illness. The couple had been told by Mark's doctor that he had an inoperable brain tumor and were given a time frame of up to one year for him to live. Venus shared with the group how they had spent those precious months together, laughing at some things, crying about others. When Mark lost his eyesight, they sadly began to discuss his funeral arrangements and Venus's life after his death, for they knew the end was drawing near. Mark didn't want Venus to be present when he passed away because he wanted her to remember him as he once was—handsome, muscular, athletic, and,

in his words, "large and in charge." He told her how much joy
their marriage had brought him, and humorously warned her
not to "rush into another marriage." Together they planned
his funeral: He wanted to be buried in a white suit and
wanted her to wear white as well. Although Venus maintained a bedside vigil toward the end, she recalled that she'd
stepped out of his hospital room for just a brief period, and
when she returned he'd slipped away. Venus smiled through
her tears and said, "He just had to have it his way." But she
concluded that the pre-death period had allowed them to
plan and prepare for his end and the beginning of her life
without him.

Roland realized he was afraid of devising a plan for his
life. "How do I make such a plan? I don't know where or how
to begin."

"Take it one day at a time," Venus told him.

The pre-death period can be used as a time to cry and a
time to set things in order as much as is possible. I encouraged Roland to talk with his young children about their
mother's illness and to prepare them for her permanent physical absence from their life.

Again, we must look at how African Americans deal with
children during the pre-death period. Our children are now
experiencing death in a very up-close-and-personal way, and

too often without guidance or direction about how to grieve. African Americans must learn to utilize the therapy and grief counseling that are available for our children. Roland's children knew only that "Mommy is sick." He'd always held out hope to them that she was going to get better. When she died, he didn't know how to explain death, and he was of little help to them because of his own deep-seated grief. Whenever possible, dying parents should be given the opportunity to have an "exit conversation" with their young children so that they can express their eternal love and give the children words of guidance and direction. Such a talk can, to some degree, help a child understand and accept the process of dying.

I remember, for example, the occasion when a beautiful, thirteen-year-old girl was taken to see her mother, Lucia, a single parent who was dying of colon cancer. Lucia was strong and ready to be relieved of her pain and suffering and to accept her own death, but she wanted to say good-bye to her daughter, whom she affectionately called "Doll." Lucia told Doll that she wouldn't be around to see her grow up, but that she'd be in heaven looking down at her, and she admonished her daughter to be "a good little girl" and to obey her grandmother, who would become her guardian. She also spoke of her wish that Doll do well in school and make something of her life. When Doll asked her mother why she had to die,

Lucia's response was "You'll die some day, too, and then we'll be together again."

Doll is now an independent twenty-one-year-old woman pursuing her career as a medical assistant. She believes that her last conversation with her mother has kept her focused. She unashamedly swears that she still feels her mother watching over and protecting her.

When Roland brought his children to a few counseling sessions, I referred to Doll's experience and asked them to share their feelings about their mother's death. They weren't clear about where Mommy was because they hadn't been allowed to attend her funeral or to view her remains. I suggested that Roland take them to the cemetery and let them lay flowers on her grave. I encouraged him to keep her memory alive for them in a loving way by looking at family photos and recounting the good times they'd shared. Children love to hear stories about their birth and how they were as babies. Soon Roland began to find healing in storytelling sessions with his children. He has a long journey before him, but at last he's on the path to grief recovery. He now regrets not using the pre-death period as a time for preparation, but, as Venus said, "the future is now!"

• • •

I'VE BEEN called on many times in my career to tell a person he or she has a terminal illness. Reflecting on those encounters, I remember Dinah Washington's recording of the song "What a Difference a Day Makes." In almost all cases, the dying patient's main desire was to experience the events of just one day. For instance, one dying mother just wanted to live to see her son graduate from college, another wanted to live to see her first grandchild, just once, while yet another only wanted to see her daughter have a beautiful wedding. Just one day is all they wanted, not a lifetime, just one day! What lesson is there in this? I believe it's that we should all learn to find joy in each day as it comes, celebrate with family and friends, build good memories daily to remember and to be remembered by those who survive us.

Many people, when they're facing death, express their feelings, fears, and wishes through poetry. One such powerful poem was recently sent to me via e-mail. The author is unknown, but I'd gladly give him or her credit for writing these words for the living.

WHEN TOMORROW
STARTS WITHOUT ME

When tomorrow starts without me, and I am not
    there to see,

If the sun should rise and find your eyes all filled
> with tears for me,
I wish so much you wouldn't cry the way you did
> today,
While thinking of the many things we didn't get to
> say.
I know how much you love me, I know you'll miss
> me too.
But when tomorrow starts without me, please try to
> understand
That an angel came and called my name and took
> me by the hand,
And said my place is ready in heaven far above,
And that I'd have to leave behind all those I dearly
> love.
But as I turned to walk away, a tear fell from my
> eye,
For all my life, I'd always thought I didn't want to die.
I had so much to live for, so much yet to do,
It seemed almost impossible that I was leaving you.
I thought of all the yesterdays, the good ones and
> the bad,
I thought of all the love we shared, and all the fun
> we had.

If I could relive yesterday, just even for a while,

I'd say goodbye and kiss you and maybe see you
  smile.

But then I fully realized that this could never be,

For emptiness and memories would take the place
  of me.

And when I thought of worldly things I might miss
  come tomorrow,

I thought of you, and when I did, my heart was
  filled with sorrow.

But when I walked through heaven's gates, I felt so
  much at home,

When God looked down and smiled on me from
  his great golden throne.

He said, "This is eternity, and all I've promised you.

Today your life on earth is past, but here it starts
  anew.

I promise no tomorrow, but today will always last.

And since each day's the same day, there's no
  longing for the past.

But you have been so faithful, so trusting and so
  true,

Though there were times you did some things you
  knew you shouldn't do.

But you have been forgiven and now at last you're
free
So won't you take my hand and share my life with
me?"
So when tomorrow starts without me, don't think
we're far apart,
For every time you think of me, I'm right there in
your heart.

AUTHOR UNKNOWN

❋

Lessons in Healing

- Allow dying loved ones to express feelings and emotions, and to say farewell to those who will live on.
- Don't neglect your children in order to care for a dying spouse, and don't shut them out by denying the reality of the inevitable.
- Never confuse dependency with love or selfishly mourn your loss at the expense of the dying.
- Speak to your loved one, even if you think he can't hear you, and express your love and gratitude aloud before it's too late.

HEALING WORDS

Today I will welcome the opportunity to give thanks to someone whose life has touched mine, and show my gratitude. I have the promise that if I am grateful over a few things, I will be entrusted with greater things. Let my attitude of gratitude begin!

❋

Good Grief, or Death as Release from Suffering

Free at last!

Sometimes, when a loved one has suffered for an extended period of time, death can provide a release not only for the person who is gone, but also for those who are left and who are relieved from the anguish of having to stand by helplessly as witnesses to his or her pain. But, as liberating as death can be for survivors in this situation, they each still need to acknowledge the hurt he or she quite naturally feels after the passing of one held so dear, and to go through the normalcy of mourning. In most cases it's impossible to bypass grief altogether, and by denying it initially the survivor is only postponing the inevitable.

That's exactly what happened to Bennet, a youthful

sixty-one-year-old man whose wife, Georgia, had died after a long and terrible illness during which she could do no more than lie, completely unresponsive, in a fetal position. Bennet hated seeing what the illness had done to his wife, and when she finally—and to his mind mercifully—died, he showed no emotion whatsoever. He failed to either admit to himself or verbalize to others how he felt about her passing. He failed to grieve her loss, and, as a result, he sank into deep depression.

In counseling, he participated in a group made up of others who, like him, were confused by the good and subsequent bad feelings they were experiencing following the death of their loved ones. They shared their personal stories, discussing the relief they'd felt when the people they'd cared about had finally been released from their suffering. What none of them had realized, however, is that some form of grieving is necessary if the survivor is to move on with his life. And gradually, they were also able to admit that their relief had left them feeling guilty. Once Bennet and the others in his group were able to release their emotions and shed the tears they'd been holding back, they were on the road to healing and recovery.

We African Americans pride ourselves on being able to go with the flow and, even after the death of a loved one, many survivors are likely to proclaim that they're alright or feel obligated to nod in agreement when a would-be consoler says, "He's better off now." But in fact, despite the mourner's relief that his loved one is no longer suffering, it's necessary for him to put voice to the feelings of sadness he will naturally feel after such a loss.

When you've done all you can for a loved one, however, and enjoyed the times you've shared, feelings of guilt will be minimal and regrets few. At times like this, African Americans with a strong spiritual base often take comfort in the biblical verse that says, "Blessed are they that die in the Lord" (Rev. 14:13, KJV).

One who managed to find such solace after both witnessing the pain of her loved one's suffering and experiencing the good grief of his release, was my friend Adriene, who lived with death on a daily basis for almost eleven months as cancer slowly took the life of her forty-five-year-old only son, Larry.

Adriene was a supervisor for a telecommunications company and had lived a modest life. A hardworking, mild-mannered sixty-five-year-old whose silver hair belied her unparalleled strength, she spoke very little about her background and, when pressed for details, usually replied, "Honey, that's all in the past. I'm just living life now day by day." That was her style—a no-nonsense individual who was known for minding her own business.

We met when I was living in Washington, D.C., and formed a lasting friendship. Because we were both mothers of only sons, we enjoyed our "brag sessions," telling each other we had the best sons in the world. We'd both worked hard to put our boys through college and were proud of their accomplishments.

Larry was "tall, light, and handsome" and loved to have a good time. He loved sports, music, and, above all, a good party. He worked for an NFL franchise, traveled extensively, and enjoyed his job immensely. He was married for a short time but, when it ended, he happily returned to the role of "momma's boy," vowing never to marry again. Although both Adriene and Larry were fiercely independent, they were bonded by mutual love, support, and sharing. Adriene's nickname for him was Brown Sugar.

A good son, Larry had always told Adriene he'd take care of her when she grew old. As an ongoing joke between them, she'd always replied, "When I can't take care of myself, I want to leave here."

When he became ill, he'd been living alone, and Adriene insisted that he move into her house "until he'd recuperated."

He received radiation and chemotherapy on an outpatient basis, but his condition only grew worse until, finally, his doctors concluded there was nothing more they could do for him.

Adriene began to grieve for all his unfulfilled dreams and to mourn the anticipated loss of her only son. Preachers and priests prayed for a miracle of healing, but it was not meant to be. Adriene cried in the bathtub, she cried while driving to the hospital, she cried when pain caused tears to run down Larry's once-handsome face. She cried at the sight of his once-sexy masculine body bloated with fluid. She cried until there were no more tears left, and then she prayed: "Take him, Lord, don't let him suffer any more."

IN CERTAIN African American circles, once it's determined that a person is going to die, the visits, phone calls, and inquiries about the patient's health become fewer and farther between. Friends and associates often feel at a loss for words of comfort and inspiration to extend to the family, and soon-to-be-survivors like Adriene are left to struggle, almost alone, in a state of functional grief. Although there are certainly more dramatic ways to die, a lengthy illness mandates that the family must contend with uncertainty, relapses, and the progressive deterioration of the patient, who is often thought of as "the living dead."

Adriene recalls one of Larry's friends reporting to others after a brief bedside visit, "He might as well be dead. He's just that bad off." She began to wish for her son's death, because she knew he was much too proud to want to be remembered as "a mere shadow of his former self."

THROUGH IT all, she maintained her abiding faith in God and privately rejoiced at the anticipation of Larry's entrance into heaven. She felt good because she knew that he himself had no fear of death. She spoke to me of the time when his doctor had told him his condition was terminal. Larry had just shrugged and said, "Hey, that's life. When it's your time to go, you gotta go."

Adriene herself was both philosophical and spiritual in her outlook. Whenever she was asked how she could stand to go to the hospital and just sit there day after day, she was never at a loss for an answer. "That's my child," she'd state with pride, "and he'd do the same thing for me." To others she might say, echoing what our black forefathers moaned in times of sorrow, "God never puts more on you than you can bear."

People who must bear witness to the prolonged terminal illness of a loved one can be in danger of having their emotions and energy drained while the recipient is incapable of giving anything back. Adriene, however, was constantly re-energized by her faith in God.

TOO OFTEN, we fail the faith test because we simply can't accept the fact that bad things do happen to good people, and that death will come to us all. Pre-denial of an impending death is unhealthy for those in the throes of anticipatory grieving, regardless of their faith or belief in miracles, because in these cases death is inevitable and only its timing is uncertain.

Whether the patient or the patient's loving family, we African Americans can be defiant in our denial. "I'm not going to die. I'm going to beat this cancer," my friend Florence vowed. But, regrettably, she lost that battle. The wife of a prominent pastor in Baltimore screamed uncontrollably, "He's not going to die and leave me!" But die he did.

Adriene, on the other hand, saw the good side of death.

When Larry died, she felt good that her son had not died from drugs, or in prison, or under other tragic circumstances. She felt good that his life had touched the lives of many young black boys and men, and that he had been an inspiration to them. She saw her son free from pain and suffering. She saw him relieved of the burden he felt his illness had placed on her. And all of that was sad . . . but it was also good.

During slavery and other hard times, black mothers who lost their sons were not afforded the luxury of taking time off from other responsibilities for a period of grieving. They did, however, find strength and comfort in the thought that "he was here for a reason, and for a season, so his living was not in vain." Adriene believed strongly that "the Lord giveth, and the Lord taketh away." God had given her the gift of Larry, and then had released him from a life of suffering by "taking him" out of his misery.

THE RELEASE of a dying loved one after long suffering can bring relief and allow the mourner to begin reconstructing his or her own life without having to go through a period of extreme grief. Adriene was standing by Larry's bed when he breathed his last. She swears she saw a faint smile cross his lips when he closed his eyes, and she likes to say he looked as if "he didn't have a care in the world."

Much to her own surprise, Adriene didn't cry. Rather she breathed a sigh of relief. "He's gone to a better place" were her words of personal consolation. She gave Larry a simple but dignified funeral and was regal through it all. Many of her friends were disappointed by her choice of a closed casket, because black folks love to "view the remains." But Adriene wouldn't put what remained of Larry on public display; he would remain forever in her heart, her thoughts, and her memory as he was in life, not death, vibrant and loved.

Because people knew of her special love for her only son, they expected her to "carry on" at the funeral and encouraged her in advance to "let it all out, cry, don't hold it in," but Adriene had already "been there, done that." She knew that no amount of crying would bring Larry back, nor would she have wanted him to live with no hope of recovery.

ADRIENE ASKED me to deliver the eulogy for Larry, and I spoke from Psalms 90:12 (KJV), which reads, "So teach us to number our days, that we may apply our hearts unto wisdom."

I reflected on Larry's God-given days, which had expanded into productive years, and spoke of the lessons life had taught him. I also alluded to the need for all those of us who are yet alive to seek wisdom from God about how to live and how to be prepared to die. In my conclusion, I addressed those who mourned the briefness of Larry's life by relating an experience from my own life. I told of being the younger of two sisters and always having to go to bed before my older sister, Willida. I had always complained bitterly about this inequity until one day, out of her frustration, my sister replied, "What are you fussing about? We both have to get up at the same time!" I told the congregation of assembled mourners that, to me, Willida's comment meant that, although Larry had died while in his prime, we who believe in the resurrection will rise when Larry arises in the glory of God, and there we will reside together as heavenly beings in heavenly bodies for all eternity.

I closed by reading a poem whose words, Adriene told me, voiced Larry's sentiments about his life and his life hereafter.

Don't grieve for me, for now I'm free,
I'm following the path God laid for me.
I took His hand when I heard him call.
I turned my back and left it all.

I could not stay another day,

To laugh, to love, to work or play.

Tasks left undone must stay that way.

If my parting has left a void,

Then fill it with remembered joy,

A friendship shared, a laugh, a kiss.

Oh, yes! These I too shall miss.

Be not burdened with times of sorrow,

I wish you the sunshine of tomorrow.

My life's been full, I savored much,

Good friends, good times, a loved one's touch.

Perhaps my time seemed all too brief,

Don't lengthen it now with undue grief.

Lift up your heart and share with me,

God wanted me now,

He set me free!

Now, when Adriene gives way to silent tears, her comfort comes from the true meaning of anticipated victory, as voiced by the late Dr. Martin Luther King, Jr., who loudly proclaimed shortly before his death:

Free at last, free at last,
Thank God almighty, I'm free at last!

※

LESSONS IN HEALING

- Caring for the dying can be emotionally and physically draining. Allow your faith in God to return the strength and energy your loved one no longer can provide.
- Do not deny the inevitable, and look upon this death as a relief from suffering for the one you loved.

HEALING WORDS

I see the need to straighten and strengthen my daily walk with the Creator so that I'll be blessed.

✳

SEVEN

Grieving Violent Death

And the earth also was corrupt before God, and
the earth was filled with violence.

GENESIS 6:11

Surely the African American community has known more than its share of violent death. Years ago, blacks understood that a fight involving "a little black eye or bloody nose" would most often resolve a dispute. Now, however, it seems that guns and other weapons of destruction have replaced fist-fighting and nonviolent mediation as the way to settle a score, and thousands of innocent lives are being lost as a result. Parents are losing children to gang-related violence, and children are losing parents to violent domestic rage. In most instances, these are senseless deaths because the warriors are almost always also the victims.

Whether it is ultimately ruled a homicide or justifiable homicide, death by violent means is a growing concern within the African American community. An alarming number of unarmed black men, and in some cases women, have been killed by police officers who claim the victim was acting suspiciously, disobeyed a command, or bore some physical re-semblance to a known suspect. According to the statistics released by many antiviolence task forces, more African Americans are murdered in most urban areas than any other ethnic group. Unfortunately, there is no indication that this kind of madness will cease. "Violence begets violence," old black folks used to say, while still others believed that "like the Bible says, 'if you live by the sword, you'll die by the sword.' " And, sad to say, the families of these victims do not always re-ceive the kind of sympathy and support they need from the community at such a time.

Violent death is never acceptable to the survivors, who respond with feelings of hate, anger, and a deep sense of rage. This kind of death raises questions of why and what-if to an entirely new level, and, unfortunately, it is usually someone close to the victim who can provide the only answer. For sur-vivors, however, the lament is most often "if only": *If only he hadn't joined a gang. If only he had stayed at home. If only she'd kept her mouth shut.*

To compound their pain, the healing process is usually delayed by lengthy investigations and legal proceedings. Luckily, in many urban areas, there are support groups where the families of victims can meet other people in similar situations, share their feelings, and receive understanding, sympathy, and grief counseling. It's sad but true, however, that a majority of African Americans resist this kind of counseling for both personal and ethnically rooted reasons. Because the primary grievers are so often incapable of providing a reasonable explanation for the tragedy, they are more likely to pledge themselves "to keep hate alive" for as long as they live, than they are to "keep hope alive." Their desire for vengeance and retribution far outweighs their desire for counseling that's aimed at addressing the issues of complicated and magnified grieving.

THE BIBLICAL story of David, chronicled in the book of Second Samuel, 19:4, tells of David's anger and grief over the death of his beloved son Absalom and records his cry, "Oh! Absalom my son, would God I had died for thee." Because of his anger, grief, and pain, the scripture says, "David mourned every day for his son." Like most parents, David assumed his son would outlive him, so Absalom's death in the prime of his life at the hands of an enemy caused David almost unbearable anger and grief.

When a child is lost to violent death, be it a police killing, a gang-related killing, or an act of domestic violence, African American parents grieve differently than they would in other circumstances. In these circumstances, the grief experience is compounded by anger, pain, and often embarrassment.

I'd venture to say that virtually every urban city has a version of my client Charlotte, a black, thirty-eight-year-old single mother of three children, each of whom has a different "out of sight, out of mind" father. Charlotte worked hard at a minimum-wage job and lived in a deteriorating housing project with her two boys, eighteen-year-old "Mookie" and sixteen-year-old "Mad Dog," and her daughter, thirteen-year-old "Lady." Mookie, tall, lanky, and arrogant, had dropped out of school and chose to run the street with a wild bunch of his notorious peers. Charlotte had been to juvenile court with him on at least six occasions, and all the court did was to send him back home. She thought the authorities should have helped him in some way. Mookie wanted to deal drugs on a small scale and use the profits to "git out of the f——g projects," as he put it, and have a bedroom of his own. Charlotte said she'd tried to talk to him and get him to return to school, but whenever she brought up the subject, her words fell on Mookie's deliberately deafened ears. She knew he was "into something," but she didn't know to what extent, and now she wonders if she really wanted to know. Mookie sometimes gave her money to help with the bills and was good to his sister and brother, but he indulged himself the most. He had a diamond stud in his ear, a collection of designer sneakers, and a CD player. He also had a beeper, and whenever it went off, he would tell his mother he had "some business to take care of."

On a brisk Saturday night in October, Mookie was killed in a drug-related shootout less than three blocks from home. Charlotte recalls a neighbor banging on her door, screaming, "Mookie's been shot!" Charlotte's face hardened with hatred and anger as she told of arriving at the crime scene and being prevented by the police from approaching her child's body. "People seemed more interested in looking at his dead body than they were in allowing me to be with my child," she said, bitterly.

Charlotte's initial grieving was delayed because the police took her home and questioned her harshly about her son's activities and his associates, making her feel as if she were his partner in crime. Then, her mourning was further compromised because she was faced with the expense of a funeral;

since she had no life insurance for either herself or her children, she had to pay cash for the burial. She received very little financial assistance from either family or friends, and she was embarrassed that she wasn't able to "put him away nicely."

She was further embarrassed by the way the media characterized her son. Mookie was described as a small-time drug dealer who was shot and killed by an unknown assailant during a drug dispute. Charlotte spoke of him as only a broken-hearted mother can. Now that he was dead, she saw only his good qualities and had begun to experience feelings of guilt for not having been able to move her family out of the projects. She'd become convinced that the neighborhood hoodlums were a bad influence on Mookie, and, therefore, the neighborhood and its hoodlums had to share some of the blame for his death.

For African Americans whose loved ones have been murdered, anger, shame, and blame are all-too-familiar emotions, and, in the long run, it becomes virtually impossible for them to grieve with dignity. Charlotte, for example, told me how disappointed she was by what she saw as a less than whole-hearted attempt on the part of the police to find her son's killer. Many blacks find it difficult to comprehend why fictional detectives and police departments, such as those depicted on shows like "NYPD Blue," "Law and Order," and my own favorite, "Columbo" are always successful in bringing the criminal to justice when, in real life, cases like Mookie's most often go unsolved.

A line from a song in the 1970s movie *Midnight Cowboy*—"Everybody's talking at me. I don't hear a word they say, only the echoes of my mind"—describes the mind-set of many of the African Americans I counsel. Charlotte was listening to but not hearing the recommended formula for her emotional healing. The only way I managed to penetrate the barrier she'd set up was to remind her that she was still the mother of two living children, and that she was failing to assist them in their own grief and anger over Mookie's death. I also suggested that to provide them with the comfort and direction they needed she'd have to relinquish her own selfish mode of grieving. Charlotte had to see that she was allowing her life to be taken over by her son's death, and that she needed to regain control and strive to achieve more structure for her family's future.

Even years after the death, African Americans continue to mourn a victim of violence using phrases like "they killed him," or "my husband was murdered," when differently worded descriptions might be "my son was the victim of a tragic act of violence," or "my husband lost his life as the result of an unfortunate confrontation." By making this minor adjustment, the survivor is able to reconstruct the memory of a loved one's death so that, over a period of time, both the victim's life and his manner of death become less painful to recall.

Charlotte did make some positive adjustments in her life. She started to show her children more attention, and her daughter was delighted when the family began to function more as a unit. Charlotte kept a tighter rein on her younger son than she had on Mookie, encouraging him to participate in supervised community activities and to do better in school. My formula for healing also included suggesting that she hug and touch her surviving children more, and that they all find good things to remember about Mookie. Towards the end of her thirteen counseling sessions, Charlotte was able to acknowledge that his involvement with drugs had played a role in Mookie's premature death. "If only..." she sighed, and I knew the end of that unfinished sentence.

ALTHOUGH CHARLOTTE'S story is typical of too many single-parent African American families struggling to get by in cities across the country, violent death visits people of all economic backgrounds and needn't be the result of either poverty or criminal behavior on the part of the victim.

I recall vividly the upper-class black family whose daughter, a college student living out of state, was killed by drug addicts who robbed her, took her car and credit cards, and left her body in a secluded area.

After not being able to reach her for more than twenty-four hours, the young woman's parents attempted to file a missing-persons report with the police in the city where she was living. But they were told they would have to wait a full forty-eight hours before the police could intervene. The mother knew in her heart that something was wrong. Sometimes we African Americans seem to be endowed with anticipatory grief. We swear we can feel death in our bones! This mother just knew her child was in danger. She felt it and was angry in advance that she couldn't convince the police to take action. When her daughter's body was discovered after eight days, her anger was compounded and uncontrolled. She was angry at her daughter's death, angry at the horrible way she'd died, angry at the police for not undertaking an immediate search, angry at the "animals" who had killed her child, angry at her husband for allowing the girl to go to college out of state, and angry at God, who had allowed this to happen.

The woman's husband prevailed upon me to visit and counsel his wife at their home, even though it would require me to travel several hours, because he believed that my meeting with her was his last hope of help. She wouldn't leave home for any reason and had shut down completely. She would not accept medication and had just let herself go. She refused to relinquish her anger, or even to reflect on pleasant memories of her daughter.

I knew of this case because of the publicity it had received, but I didn't know the family personally and was, therefore, a bit surprised to learn I'd been recommended by a mutual professional acquaintance. Nevertheless, I agreed to the visit, and when I arrived I found a beautiful house that was no longer a home, but rather a shrine to the deceased.

The mother obviously resented my very presence and the purpose for which I had come. When I chose a seat, she hollered, "DON'T SIT THERE!" and proceeded to physically remove me from the chair, telling me it was where her daughter always sat. When I asked her if she thought her daughter would object to my sitting in that chair if she were alive, the woman was incensed at the very suggestion that her daughter would have been so rude and ill-mannered. "She wasn't like that," was her response. I then asked if she thought her daughter would want her to "act like that," and at that point she broke down and cried. When her husband attempted to hold her, she pushed him away.

"Don't you understand?" she wailed. "My baby is dead— she was killed, she was tortured, and she probably tried to fight them off. Why didn't she just give them what they wanted? But no, she's just like her father; nobody takes nothing from them without a fight." Now she was displaying unjustified anger at her daughter, even in death.

After that, she cried and talked, recounting every detail she could recall, but only about the way her daughter had died, as if there had been no life before her death. (And, by the way, I did sit in that chair.)

I later found out that this was her first opportunity to talk uninterruptedly and without comment on the part of her listener. Up until then, she said, whenever she'd become hysterical, someone had tried to silence her, comfort her, or pray for her. Well-meaning folk had even said they "knew how she felt." I listened intently while she cursed and screamed, until finally she was physically exhausted and emotionally drained. I asked for something to drink, which called for a move from the sitting area to her lovely kitchen, where she and I were out of earshot of her husband.

She then wondered aloud, "How can anyone expect me to get over this? I can't!"

I reminded her that her daughter's death was over, the funeral was over, and nothing would change that. I reminded
her of several well-known African American personalities
who had suffered tragic losses of children. The murder of the
son of comedian and television star Bill Cosby and his wife,
Camille, on a deserted highway, came to mind, along with the
death by drowning of the son of the famous basketball star
Julius Irving (Dr. J) and his wife, Turquoise. After their son,
who had a history of drug abuse, had been missing for several days, his body was found in his car, submerged in a small
lake not far from their Florida home.

I then talked about other, not so well-known parents who
had also lost children in tragic and violent circumstances. She
listened and momentarily connected with the anger and loss
that, luckily, only a few of us know by actual experience.

She was surprised when I began to quote back to her,
word for word, some of the angry words she had spoken. I
had taken no notes, and she was impressed that I had not
only listened but also *heard* what she had said, and she
seemed to know the difference.

At some point, in her anger, she had spoken of her desire (and ability) to kill those who had murdered her daughter. I felt it imperative to point out to her how anger can
reduce us to the level of the one who is the source of our

anger. If, in fact, she took the opportunity to "kill the killers," I told her, she would also be a murderer and would have to suffer the consequences of her deed. In addition to which, the death of the murderers would not restore her daughter's life.

She had also expressed her desire to see the killers die in the electric chair, and had stated that she would gladly pull the switch. I then discussed with her the difference between the death of the body and the death of the spirit of a loved one. Death cannot kill the spirit, nor does it kill our memory of the departed, and anger should not be permitted to deprive us of the joy and comfort those memories can bring. I agreed with her statement that "nothing would ever be the same," but encouraged her to realize that she would eventually learn to cope with the ways in which her life had changed.

EVEN WHEN people are angry with God, they maintain the hope of a residence in God's heaven for their loved one. Most of us believe that heaven is the final destination and resting place for all good people, and we believe that when we die, we will be reunited with our loved ones in heaven. Unlike the Catholic religion, which embraces a belief in purgatory, a place to purge the sins we have committed in life, the

Christian faith teaches that the passage from earth to glory is a nonstop trip. This mother was confident that her daughter was, indeed, in heaven, but she was still angry. We discussed her concept of heaven as it related to her daughter, and she smiled and said, "I bet she's giving them a fit up there." That reflection and smile were a breakthrough for her.

It's important to remember that the Creator never promised us a grief-free life, but neither should we grieve without the hope of a better life after death, which is a spiritual one, without pain or suffering. Indeed, a part of that mother did die with her daughter, but I reminded her of the many aspects of her life that were still in place. For she was not only her daughter's mother, she was also a woman, a wife, and a daughter herself. She was educated and had enjoyed success in her profession of choice, and she was a valuable asset to her civic and church communities.

I spoke of a book by Jill Brooke entitled *Don't Let Death Ruin Your Life*. The title alone, I suggested, should be a challenge to the griever to live out the remainder of his or her life without the daily presence of the departed loved one. There is no joy in being around the "living dead," and life mandates interaction with living beings. I referred back to the chair she hadn't wanted me to sit in and told her that she didn't need that chair to remind her of her daughter. Objects are not people, and objects have no life. To begin healing from anger, don't just cherish and enshrine the things of the departed. If being surrounded by those things triggers your anger, get rid of them, use them, or rearrange them, and celebrate the joy those things gave your loved one.

In this case, I suggested she vent her anger in the right direction, and use its passion to bring about positive change in the area of drug use among African American youths and young adults. African Americans are now becoming more involved in social change, especially in situations referred to as "unnecessary deaths." Mothers Against Drunk Driving (MADD) is an organization that came into being as the result of the anger of parents whose children had been killed in alcohol-related auto accidents. Their anger has produced a great benefit; laws with severe penalties for drunk drivers now exist, and those laws have saved many lives.

Similarly, Megan's Law, which requires local registration and notification of sex offenders released from prison and residing in any neighborhood, was enacted as the outcome of the efforts of outraged parents whose little girl had been the victim of a vicious and fatal sexual assault.

Positive anger has also brought national attention to unwanted babies being suffocated at birth, and has resulted in the passage of laws that allow such newborns to be left at hospitals without any penalty for the parent.

As a people, we believe strongly in the living spirit of our deceased loved ones, and we must, therefore, take care not to cause those spirits to grieve for our displays of anger over their death. We should consider that, as we grieve for their passing, so do they grieve for the anger it has caused us to feel.

We speak of our loss, but we must remember that our loss is not lost, for, while we feel the void left by our loved one's absence, St. Paul the Apostle says in Second Corinthians 5:6 that "to be absent from the body is to be present with the Lord." When mourners accept the fact that the spirit of their lost loved one is at peace and under the protection of the Creator, little by little their anger subsides.

Some time after my visit, I received a beautiful gift and a lovely card from this mother telling me that she was "getting stronger," had resumed some of her activities, and was working with a support group in her area for parents whose children had been murdered. She had told her story publicly before a group of these parents and talked about her struggle to release herself from anger. She let them know that when her intense anger ended after two years, she began to live life differently, accepting the things she could not change and effecting change where she could. This mother now has good days, and the bad days are becoming just not-so-good days. The good days outnumber the bad, and she can state with conviction that "God is still good."

THE FACT that violence is an "equal-opportunity killer" was brought home to me yet again when my dear friend and professional colleague, Betty Martin Blount, R.N.C.S., M.S.N., Ed.D., asked me to act as co-counselor with her on a particularly difficult and disturbing case. Dr. Blount, a certified psychotherapist, is the Director of Blount & Odum Christian Counseling Associates in Philadelphia and is known as "the counselor's counselor" because of her many years of experience in the field. As a grief-counseling specialist, her innovative techniques serve as a model for many African American grief counselors. I'm proud to say that we've worked together on many difficult and challenging cases and she has always proved to be a true professional and a treasured friend.

One of our most challenging co-ventures involved the murder of a vivacious thirty-three-year-old woman named Karen, who'd seemed to "have it all." Both her parents were professionals enjoying successful and financially rewarding careers. Karen and her siblings were typical upper middle class African American children. Their parents knew that they were spoiled, but that they were also smart. They had been motivated by their mother and father always to reach for the better things in life. Karen graduated with honors from a leading university and was accepted into medical school, where she began to pursue her dream of becoming a gynecologist. During her internship at a city hospital, she met and fell madly in love with a handsome thirty six year old man whose many character flaws she, in her infatuation, overlooked. However, when Karen introduced Devon to her family, her older sister, Cathy, disliked him immediately. Pressed for a reason, she said only, "He has cold and cruel looking eyes."

Devon was the product of a dysfunctional family. His father was an alcoholic with abusive tendencies, and his mother tolerated her husband's abuse until he died at the age of fifty eight. Devon wasn't close to his family, and so, as their relationship developed, he and Karen became virtually inseparable. His life centered entirely on her, and she was mesmerized and flattered by the attention.

After an eleven month courtship, Devon and Karen were married, much to her family's disappointment. Just a few months into the marriage, however, Karen began to feel smothered by Devon's possessive and controlling behavior, and Devon sensed her resentment. Their constant arguing escalated into physical fights from which Karen emerged with swollen eyes and bruises all over her body. She lied to her family and co-workers about the cause of her injuries and vehemently denied that she was being physically abused by her husband.

Cathy begged her sister to leave Devon, but Karen ignored her pleas and indicated that, although the marriage was not without problems, she and Devon were trying to work things out.

Details of the final argument that resulted in Karen's death are yet unknown, but neighbors reported having heard her screaming in pain and pleading for her life. The police were called and discovered Karen's bloody, beaten body on the bed. Devon was sitting in a chair crying uncontrollably. Of course he was arrested and charged with her murder. But that was only the beginning of a long period of recovery from the total devastation this act of madness had wrought on Karen's family, all of whom became caught up in a cycle of trauma-related grieving. They were fully aware of what had caused their grief, but they could see no way to recover from their pain.

· · ·

THE GRIEVING family was referred to Dr. Blount by a dear friend who was concerned about their mental, emotional, and physical well-being. Individually and collectively they had lost their zest for life, and now all they had in common was the grief they shared. Years ago, it would have been customary for an African American father to approach an abusive son-in-law and offer to give him "a dose of his own medicine" if he ever laid hands on his daughter again. Or a brother, an uncle, or a male cousin would have "paid a visit" to the abuser, thus ending the husband's abusive behavior. Strong black mothers and grandmothers in days long gone also acted as defenders of their daughters and other abused women. Black women with violent companions were taught to fight back in ways that would ensure a rapid end to any further physical attacks. Their unique methods consisted of disarming the abuser with a generous sprinkling of cayenne pepper aimed at his eyes, or a good dousing with boiling water, and, of course, a swift and powerful kick to the man's "jewel box," located below the belt. These actions, coupled with ongoing monitoring of the relationship by concerned family members, usually proved to be effective deterrents to further altercations. As a last resort, the wife might have been moved back home by her father, with a warning to the husband of the consequences he could expect if he dared "even dart the steps" of the family home.

Time, however, has brought about a change in the way African Americans deal with abuse, and for some strange reason, many modern black women—like their white counterparts—now tolerate spousal abuse "for the sake of the children," or for the comforts provided by combined incomes. Since the recognition of abuse as a criminal act, many women—black and white alike—now choose to rely on police intervention when a physical fight occurs, or they wait for a courtroom judge to mete out meager punishment (unfortunately, usually probation).

Karen's family had taken a hands-off approach to her troubled marriage in the belief that she knew they were there for her if she wanted or needed their help. Now her father felt guilty because of his decision not to intervene. And her mother blamed herself for not recognizing the warning signs of her daughter's fear. Neither parent had made any effort to recover from their grief; instead, they chose deliberately to recall all the morbid details of Karen's death and to make them a part of their daily life.

In addition, they had lost touch with their own spiritual beliefs and only wanted an acceptable answer to the question "Where was God when our daughter was being killed?" Sometimes we expect that God will provide divine intervention in any and all of life's threatening scenarios, and, in this instance, Karen's parents felt that He had failed in his godly duties.

When mourners reject spiritual consolation, they most often reject any attempt to view the tragedy from an intellectual perspective as well. To Karen's parents, their daughter's murder was totally senseless, and the craziness of the act was making them crazy.

Dr. Blount patiently guided the distraught parents through the stages of their multilevel grief, while I concentrated on dealing with the complexity of her sisters' mourning. In addition to hating Devon, Cathy was angry with herself because she thought she could have prevented Karen's death if only she'd intervened in some way. The younger sister, Kayla, was finding it difficult to move past the grotesque image she was carrying in her head of Karen's beaten and battered body. She also felt robbed of her ability to trust in a relationship, and, in a strange way, she felt like a victim, too, because, unlike Cathy, she had actually liked Devon. Now she was confused as to how he could have committed such a heinous crime, and she felt that he'd deceived her.

Although this had been a close and loving family, each surviving member was now wrapped in a personal blanket of unmanageable individual grief. Dr. Blount and I spent hours discussing and devising a grief-recovery formula for the parents and the siblings. We realized that, because of their focus on Devon's impending trial and their desire for him to receive the death penalty, their ability to grieve properly for Karen still lay in the future. They were obsessed with witnessing Devon's death by lethal injection, and when I suggested the possibility of his receiving a sentence of life imprisonment, the mere thought that he might continue to live was anathema, particularly to Karen's father who vowed, "I'll kill him myself." While it's usually futile for a counselor to try to dispel a mourner's desire for revenge, Dr. Blount and I did point out that Devon's death would never restore Karen's life.

Dr. Blount spoke candidly to the parents about what she perceived as their reluctance to let go of their bitterness and anger and urged them not to allow these negative emotions to become their way of commemorating their daughter's life. Survivors can't ignore indefinitely the demands life places upon them, and they need to achieve a level of grieving that will still allow them to function. Dr. Blount told Karen's parents that they "would never get over it," but that they could "get through it."

I counseled Cathy and Kayla not to "strive just to survive" but to "aim at achieving some small victory day by day." I shared with them a self-published book I'd written several years before, entitled *Victory Day by Day*, that contains motivational and inspirational meditations and daily affirmations for grieving. Here's the one that Cathy said spoke to her heart.

I'M IN REMISSION

Today I examine the remission process taking place in my life. I acknowledge that there are things in my life that need to decrease until they cease to exist, i.e., temper, jealousy, unkind words and thoughts, and the list goes on. Remission is not a visible process, but rather one that takes place from within, and is evidenced by ongoing recovery. I now decree, let remission begin, though gradual and perhaps with a degree of pain, I am improving from within. I now rejoice in the progression of my remission.

The family was in counseling and therapy for more than two years before they began to show signs of real progress in their healing and recovery. Ultimately, they found it impossible to heal without returning to their spiritual foundation, so they resumed praying and attending worship services.

After two long years, Devon was found guilty of Karen's murder and received a sentence of fifteen years to life. Cathy thought the penalty would have been more severe if Karen had been a white woman, but eventually she moved past her death wish for Devon.

Karen's mother was still experiencing deep sorrow, and I referred her to a lamentation of David who, in Psalms 31:9, petitioned of God:

Have mercy upon me, O Lord, for I am in trouble:
Mine eye is consumed with grief, yea, my soul and
  my belly.

And David concluded his Psalm in verse 24 by telling mourn-ers:

Be of good courage and He shall strengthen your
  heart, all ye that hope in the Lord.

❋

LESSONS IN HEALING

- Make a vow not to "keep hate alive," and seek counseling to resolve your desire for retribution.
- Learn to change the words you use when referring to violent death so that your loved one's manner of dying will become less painful to recall.
- Never allow yourself to become one of the "living dead." Use the force of your anger to bring about positive social change.
- Aim at achieving small victories day by day.

HEALING WORDS

I will not become vindictive or step out of character, for if I but appeal to my higher and inner power, I will be victorious this day, and those evil forces and thoughts will flee from me.

THE SERENITY PRAYER

Lord, grant me the serenity to accept
the things I cannot change,
To change the things I can,
And the wisdom to know the difference.

※

EIGHT

Unspeakable Deaths

DYING OF AIDS

God made no death; neither hath he pleasure in
the destruction of the living.

APOCRYPHA: WISDOM OF SOLOMON

There are still certain causes of death that make it even more difficult than usual for those left behind to express their grief, and when grief is repressed it's harder to heal and harder to let go. One death that still dare not speak its name—particularly in our community—is suicide; another—difficult as this may be for some of us to believe in this century—is AIDS. In the first instance, the guilt of the bereaved and the disapproval of the community combine to create a kind of social taboo. In the case of AIDS, the guilt falls on the shoulders of the victim, who is too often seen as "getting no more than he (or she) deserved." Differences of opinion about this deadly and horrific disease, its cause and the reasons for the disproportionately heavy toll it's taken on the African American community have created ongoing debate involving both racial discrimination issues and theologically based interpretations of scripture.

Julian Bond, the renowned civil rights activist, was quoted in an editorial in the *New York Times* discussing AIDS in the African American community as saying, point blank, "This has become a black disease" (Jan. 1, 2001). The same article then goes on to state that the Centers for Disease Control estimates that AIDS is now the leading cause of death among African Americans between the ages of twenty-five and forty-four, and that black women now account for sixty-four percent of those newly infected in the United States. And those women are passing the infection along to their children, who are dying by the thousands in infancy or early childhood.

Even now, when there are effective treatments available, many African Americans can't afford the costly medications and too frequently choose to deny their failing health to concerned family and friends. As a result, while the death rate among other populations may be going down, among blacks it is still on the rise.

AIDS IN THE GAY COMMUNITY

Too often, when a gay black male contracts the virus, his AIDS status takes precedence over every other aspect of his identity and negates all his achievements. Such was the case for Chip, a vibrant, witty, smart, lovable, and talented gay musician who died of AIDS at the age of thirty-six. Much to the distress and anger of his grieving family, for many of their friends and relatives that fact alone told the story of his whole life.

When he was diagnosed, he fought the virus with all his might, taking solace in his music and in the unconditional love of his family and a small circle of close friends until the disease had completely ravaged his body. When he finally gave up the fight and died, his parents were not prepared for the community's reaction. Some people were afraid to enter the house where Chip had lived; others were afraid to embrace his family, ignorantly believing they could "catch something." When it came time to arrange for the funeral, the family was devastated when their pastor suggested holding the service at the funeral home chapel rather than in the church. Chip's parents were active members of the congregation. Chip had grown up in the church, where he had participated in musical activities and performed as a soloist with the choir.

Chip's family was understandably angry at the pastor's reaction as well as at the church officials who concurred with his position. Many ministers within the African American community, along with other church leaders, have been extremely vocal in their condemnation of homosexuality, both from the pulpit and in print. Published articles and spirited public debate among the clergy, both black and white, have compounded the confusion surrounding biblical interpretation of this controversial subject. Many ministers are of the opinion that God uses AIDS and other calamities as instruments of punishment for sins of disobedience. One black minister has gone so far as to state that, since smoking results in death from lung cancer, and alcohol causes death from liver disease, he believes that AIDS comes from the sin of same-sex intimacy. But even if one accepted that harsh judgment, the analogy fails to address the plight of innocent parties who unknowingly have sex with an infected partner of the opposite sex who might be bisexual or an intravenous drug user.

Chip's family had noticed his "feminine ways" early in his childhood, and had discussed with him their concern as well as their confusion. When they saw that Chip was comfortable with being who he was and what he was, however, they loved him as he was, unconditionally. His family never saw him as a freak or a sissy, rather they accepted him as a talented, loving person whose sexual preference was for intimacy with other men.

When the family decided to have Chip's body cremated, their pastor criticized them again, because, he said, the Bible didn't endorse this method of disposing of the remains. Instead of a traditional funeral the family held a memorial service, forgoing the religious ritual of a pastoral eulogy. Chip's friends from the gay community performed secular music and memorialized him with glowing reflections on his life.

The pain and grief resulting from their anger brought Chip's parents into counseling. Their anger was directed both at the church and at those judgmental friends and family members who had not only abandoned Chip while he was dying, but had also turned their backs on his survivors in their time of grief. In counseling, however, they discovered that they had also been suppressing their feeling that Chip's death might have been preventable, and that this, too, was making them angry and causing them grief. For the first time, they expressed anger at Chip for indulging in unprotected sex. "At least he could have used condoms," his mother lamented. Chip's father, for the first time, voiced outrage at the partner who had infected his son and wondered aloud if the unidentified transmitter of the virus had known he was infected when he engaged in sex with Chip.

Death from AIDS is viewed by many as an unnatural death, and African American survivors often look for someone to blame for what they consider an unnecessary and avoidable loss. Because of the many unanswered questions surrounding Chip's disease and death, his parents didn't know *how* to grieve. Should they be grieving simply the loss of their son, or the cause of his death, or their own isolation, or the loss of those whom they had considered their friends? I pointed out to them that no death is ever acceptable to those who lose a loved one, and that the cause of Chip's death should not be allowed to diminish the positive aspects of his life. In counseling, they soon came to realize that they had been so preoccupied with the nature of Chip's death and with their own ostracism, that they hadn't been able to properly celebrate his life or grieve for their loss.

They also realized that they needed to find a replacement for the religious faith they'd lost as a result of the treatment they'd received by those who were "supposed to be Christians." In these situations, mourners find it difficult to separate their belief in a loving, understanding, and forgiving God from the conduct and actions of the insensitive, uncaring, and judgmental proclaimed followers of His teachings. I explained to Chip's parents that if sin is a given, meaning that all humans err, commit sinful acts, and entertain sinful and sometimes evil thoughts, then we all stand condemned. I shared with them one of the many powerful biblical discourses delivered by Christ on the subject of sin.

St. John, chapter 8 (KJV) recounts the parable of an unnamed woman caught in the act of adultery, a sin according to the laws of Moses, whose punishment should be, said her accusers, to be stoned to death. According to the scripture, Christ, upon hearing this, stooped, and wrote with his finger in the dirt. Then he rose up and uttered these words: "He that is without sin among you. Let him first cast a stone against her." One by one, her accusers disappeared, and when Christ saw that none remained to condemn her, He said to the woman, "Neither do I condemn thee. Go and sin no more." While in the eyes of some, this woman had committed an unpardonable act, she received forgiveness for her fleshly weakness and misdeeds from a kind and loving savior. Whether our actions are called sins, errors, or weaknesses of

the flesh, we need to maintain our firm belief in the unconditional understanding and forgiveness of our Creator.

In this same session, I also discussed with them the cate-
gorizing of sins by certain self-appointed judges of morality.
Is homosexuality worse than stealing? Is domestic abuse
worse than lying? I pointed out that there are consequences
to pay for all misdeeds, but we must never assume that these
consequences are acts of retribution or punishment meted
out by an angry God.

Chip's parents were eventually able to overcome their
anger and grieve without judging his sexual choices. While
they still harbored a degree of animosity toward the pastor,
church members, and others who had abandoned them in
their time of bereavement, they also wanted to move on with
their lives. They found comfort by remembering Chip in a
positive and pleasant light, and they were able to grieve the
loss of the son they had adored despite the cause of his death.

The family was embraced by Chip's gay friends who, unlike the "church folks," loved him as his parents did. They
completed counseling, pledging to seek out an understanding
pastor and congregation who "loved all of God's children," including homosexuals. And they were also determined to con-
nect with a support group for Parents of AIDS Victims,

where they would find others who, like themselves, were not ashamed of or guilty about their loved one's sexual preferences.

Chip's parents kept the urn containing his ashes on the mantel in their home, saying that it made them feel as if he were still a part of their loving family. Some months after their last counseling session, I received an invitation to a memorial musical concert in celebration of Chip's life. All proceeds from the concert were being donated to an African American program whose objective is to provide care for those living with and dying from AIDS.

As a people, we African Americans must face up to the reality of the AIDS epidemic within our community. We must, without prejudice or judgment, provide assistance to the victims and comfort to the survivors. And we must promote public awareness of the disease. Survivors of those who die of AIDS need to be able to grieve without the stigma of shame or embarrassment.

> We passed their graves;
> The dead men there,
> Winners or losers,
> Did not care.

In the dark
They could not see
Who had gained
The victory.

"PEACE," LANGSTON HUGHES

AIDS, THE SCOURGE OF BLACK WOMEN

More and more African American women are dying of AIDS, often as a result of poverty, limited education, and simply being the product of a dysfunctional family and/or dating structure. These infected females are often the victims of racism and sexism based on ignorance and widespread misconceptions about this dreaded disease. Black women with AIDS are generally assumed to be drug users or prosti-tutes, or both; however, little attention is focused on the risk women face, even in heterosexual, monogamous relationships when the men with whom they are sexually involved transmit the virus to their innocent female partners.

Toni was only twenty-four when she was diagnosed with full-blown AIDS, and the only person who grieved her death was her childhood friend, Jennie, who came to me in desper-ate need of grief counseling. Jennie told Toni's story with passionate anger and pain. At the age of nineteen she had dropped out of school and left home because of the constant turmoil within her family. "All Toni wanted was to be loved and feel she was special to someone," Jennie said. In pursuit of this love, Toni engaged in risky sexual behavior with multiple partners, totally unaware that they were just using her for their sexual pleasure.

Approximately eight months before her death, she began to develop swollen glands, diarrhea, extreme tiredness, and high fevers. Jennie insisted that Toni go to the free clinic for a checkup, and, after a series of tests, Toni was diagnosed with advanced AIDS. Jennie took it upon herself to inform Toni's family of her failing health and impending demise, but they were concerned only with concealing her condition from their neighbors and friends. They would have nothing to do with her, although Toni's mother did tell Jennie that she would see to it that her daughter had food to eat.

Toni had worked as a barmaid, and her main income came from tips. The bar where she worked didn't provide health benefits, and she was too sick to search for support services. Jennie took Toni to live with her and vowed to do all she could to help her friend.

When she was talking to me, Jennie cried about the times Toni vomited uncontrollably, cried out in pain, and, toward the end, shrank to "nothing but skin and bones." Jennie also recalled her own feelings of rage, bitterness, despair, and frustration at the injustice of Toni's plight. She was facing death and, in addition to her physical pain, she'd had to deal with the emotional trauma of an unsupportive family and the devastation of realizing that none of her male "lovers" ever came to visit her because, like too many ignorant people, they believed you could catch AIDS from casual contact.

When Toni finally died, Jennie sank into a state of complicated grief and severe depression, and she knew she needed help to get out of her downward spiral. She had to process her anger at the "ignorant black folks" who had so harshly judged and misjudged Toni; at the men who'd had sex with her but didn't give a damn about her; at the family members who were too ashamed even to attend her funeral; and finally at being stigmatized herself by association. Jennie was suffering from both pre- and post-death grieving for her friend as well as for herself. "Nobody should have to die like that, and, if it weren't for me, she would have died all alone," Jennie exclaimed. She didn't know how to get through her anger and bitterness and get on with her own life. There was no one to share her grief or to console her for the loss of her dearest friend.

African Americans often tend to distance themselves from grieving the death of someone who, in their opinion, dies a shameful death. Jennie sarcastically mimicked those people who said, "Oh, your friend died. That's a shame." "What's a shame?" Jennie was tempted to ask. It was a shame that Toni had been so isolated; it was a shame she'd been rejected by her own family; and it was a shame that, because Jennie had been exposed to AIDS through her friendship with Toni, it was assumed that, sooner or later, she too would "come down with something."

In counseling, it was apparent to me that Jennie was suffering from grief overload and needed help reviewing and revising her perception of the circumstances surrounding Toni's death. I advised her to stop trying to justify her anger and begin to grieve the loss of Toni as she would grieve any dear friend's death. She needed to acknowledge the fact that Toni was dead, let her volatile anger subside, and move on to finding a way to cope with life and the social injustices suffered by victims of AIDS, especially women.

In counseling, Jennie discovered that her grief process was also being complicated by the void any longtime caregiver experiences when he or she is no longer needed. She missed Toni's dependence and could neither understand nor explain this emptiness in her life. Jennie received a monthly

Social Security disability check for a childhood injury that had left her with a severe limp, and she had a modest inheritance from her grandmother. She didn't work and, without anything to occupy her long idle days, she was investing too much time and emotion in anger and abnormal grieving.

Jennie saw her life flash before her on a mental screen and decided she didn't like what she was seeing. As a result of her newly gained insight and past experience, she was determined to become involved in volunteer work helping women with AIDS and HIV. She now wants to become certified as an AIDS counselor and hopes one day to open a hospice-type facility in Toni's memory where African American women with AIDS are lovingly cared for and can die with dignity. She completed her counseling determined to make this dream a reality and prove that Toni's living and dying had not been in vain.

NO UNDERSTANDING
Come with me
Into my heart
To feel exactly
What I am
Feeling now.

Follow me on this
Path that has
Led me nowhere,
I have been traveling
This road for
A long time.

Come with me and
Explain this misery
That has captured
My young life,
Such a short way
Down the road,
Break it down for
Me so that I can
Understand beyond
This expulsion of anger.
I have no understanding
From failure and unmet expectations.

Nobody saw that the flame
No longer shone brightly.

CHENISE LYTRELLE

CHILDREN AND AIDS

Since the first five gay men were diagnosed with AIDS in 1981, the virus has caused the deaths of thousands of innocent babies and youths born into the African American community. Because, early on, only homosexuals and drug users who shared needles were thought to be at risk for contracting the virus, little attention was paid to the alarming number of infants and "sickly" children who were also dying. Now, of course, we know that the virus was being passed on by an AIDS-infected mother, who was often not even aware of the risk to her child.

Almost always, when a person dies, there's someone to mourn their passing. That person had a history, and someone knew his or her story. For countless African American children, however, there is no history and no one to mourn their passing. Often, the child's father is unknown, incarcerated, or already dead from the virus, and the mother has either abandoned her baby at birth or preceded him or her in death. One elderly black woman has called the AIDS deaths of black babies "a generational curse." "It's wiping us out," she said, citing as an example of what, for her, was an all-too-familiar scenario, one family in which three generations had succumbed to AIDS: a thirty-nine-year-old man who had fought "drug demons" since his teens and died after contracting the virus as a result of sharing a needle with an infected addict; the young man's eighteen-year-old daughter, who became a prostitute in order to support her own hundred-dollar-a-day drug habit; and the daughter's baby, who died at the age of three. Stories like this one abound in urban black communities across this nation and are, in fact, so common that they are no longer considered newsworthy.

My administrator, Delores, introduced me to a dear friend of many years, Mrs. Maurice McClintock, who has dedicated much of her life to being an advocate for children with AIDS in the Philadelphia area. Since retiring from her position as a personnel analyst for a major corporation, she has served on the board of the St. Mary's Family Respite Center, an organization that provides not only compassion and caring but also practical services for children and families affected by AIDS.

Another woman who could "write a book" on the lives of those affected by AIDS (if only she had the time) is Pam, a client of mine who is a social service worker with an overwhelming caseload. Pam has seen children with AIDS made wards of the court because there was no family to care for them. "They never had a life," she says sadly, "and they slowly die, a little each day." Many of these children are orphaned or abandoned by their parents and relatives and, too often, their death marks the end of the family line. While they live, however, they need to be shown all the love, support, and understanding the community can provide.

Some children who are victims of inherited AIDS have never known a pain-free day. Most die alone, in a care facility or a hospital. Pam remembers funerals with no family members present, and innocent children who are buried in unmarked graves without anyone to mourn their passing.

African Americans should begin to grieve posthumously for these precious children, for in their dying, we as a people have lost a significant part of our history and of our future as well. We cannot deny any longer the deadly impact AIDS has had on the black community, nor can we survive by remaining angry at the cause of the disease without facing up to its consequences. And if we are to save future generations of children, we must find a way to educate those who are giving birth to them, so that they won't be brought into the world only to face certain death.

IN ADDITION to the babies who have died of the disease, there are also those children who have lost parents to it, and they are victims as well. Throughout my ministry I've met many of these poor little souls, who have lived all their lives dealing with adult problems and who have had to cope with an unimaginably abnormal way of life. Children as young as five years old have had to become caregivers to mothers who are dying of AIDS and who are sometimes drug-addicted as well. There are even cases of children who have discovered their parent's body and whose unspoken shock and horror have gone totally unacknowledged and untreated. Too often these children have few if any pleasant memories and don't know how to express their feelings of grief, anger, enduring pain, and fear. They listen carefully to the comments made in their presence by insensitive adults; they learn early in life what it means to be infected with AIDS; and because they are assumed to be carriers, they are treated accordingly. Many of these children mourn with deep anger at the stigma that attaches to their parent's death.

It's an old African American proverb that told us "it takes a village to raise a child," but sadly, those villages have in recent times all but disappeared. Small, close-knit neighborhoods have been replaced by large public housing projects whose tenants hide behind locked doors. As a result, I believe it's now up to our churches and ministries to recreate that village and make caring for our children—particularly those whose lives are impacted by AIDS—the core of their concern. We must learn to show compassion for grieving children and help them through their period of mourning. Give them the opportunity to express their feelings and give vent to their emotions. Get them to draw pictures or make paintings that may speak louder and more eloquently than their childish words allow.

And, above all, because the African American community now has the highest rate of AIDS-caused deaths in the country, we must attack this virus as we would a deadly enemy!

WHEN A LOVED ONE TAKES HIS OWN LIFE

O! Jonathan! My Jonathan!

O! Jonathan! . . . I am distressed for thee . . . Very
pleasant hast thou been unto me . . . thy love to me
was wonderful . . .

EXCERPTS FROM DAVID'S LAMENTATION IN

FIRST SAMUEL 1:25–26 (KJV)

Teressa V. Staten, Ph.D, is one of America's leading reformers in education. She has been called upon to evaluate school systems and devise models for school administrators and instructors nationwide. Dr. Staten and her husband, John, a retired prison system administrator, are unapologetically upper-class African Americans whose successful careers and family life are respected and admired by all who know them. They and their family are among my dearest friends, and they have also, tragically, experienced the grief caused by the suicide of a loved one—their elder son, Johnathan, at the age of twenty-six. Teressa and John both hope that my recounting of their experience will help other parents, relatives, and friends deal with suicide and its lasting effects on bereaved survivors.

Johnathan was the older of two sons, privileged black youths who were exposed to the best life had to offer, attended the best schools, and traveled all over the world on annual family vacations. Johnathan was loving and outgoing. He excelled at sports and had many, many friends. After college, he surprised his parents by announcing that he had applied for and been given a job in the police department of the city where they lived. They'd always hoped he would become a lawyer, but they accepted his decision and were supportive of his career choice.

Johnathan was assigned to the city housing projects and received both accolades from local residents and citations from the mayor for his role in eliminating drug traffic in the neighborhoods where he worked. He established a good rapport with the youth in the projects and coached City League football teams. He treated the kids to pizza parties, helped them with their schoolwork, and even played Santa Claus at Christmas. The children adored him and his superiors held him in high esteem.

In his personal life, Johnathan was involved with an older white woman. He loved her dearly and was crazy about her young daughter, to whom he was like a father. Johnathan purchased a small house where they lived as a family for a few years until, one day, the woman abruptly severed the relationship and moved out. Johnathan was devastated and became so depressed that, without his parents' knowledge, he began to see a psychiatrist on a regular basis.

Only after his suicide did the Statens learn that just four weeks before his death, three psychiatrists had observed Johnathan and one had suggested that he keep a written journal of his daily thoughts, feelings, and activities. Teressa was stunned when, upon reading the journal, she discovered several references to suicidal thoughts and Johnathan's desire to end his life. Enraged, she confronted his primary psychiatrist, who simply indicated that he'd had a "contract" with Johnathan stating that the patient would call the doctor before he took his life.

The Statens were furious with the psychiatrists who'd

been aware of their son's suicidal thoughts and yet had never recommended that he be temporarily removed from his job and relieved of his firearm. They still believe his suicide could have been prevented. And, since becoming aware—only after his death—of the depth of his depression, they feel the doctors could have suggested he be hospitalized, or at least that he move out of the house that held such painful memories for him. They also believe that they, as his parents, or his superior officer, should have been notified of his state of mind.

The Journal of Police Science and Administration lists policing as among the most dangerous, stressful, and health-threatening occupations. It's related to high levels of alcoholism, suicide, and divorce, in addition to a variety of other stress-related physical and emotional ailments. In urban areas, the number of police officers of all races, creeds, and colors involved in murder-suicides is on the rise. African American law officers are killing themselves—and frequently a wife or lover as well.

BLACKS, AS a group, are generally both under-diagnosed and under-treated by mental health professionals, at least partly as a result of the self-perpetuating myth of "black strength."

African American males in particular have long taken pride in their ability to survive any kind of adversity, as well as in their manliness.

Stories handed down from one generation to the next tell of the "danger, toils, and snares through which we have already come." Our gospel hymns and spirituals speak of survival and chant their encouragement to "hold on just a little while longer, and a change will come." My own favorite saying on the subject of "holding on" is "if you can take it, you can make it."

Despite the fact that suicide is on the rise among black youths and young adults, most African Americans still have less confidence in psychology, psychiatry, and mental health counseling than most whites, and they tend to fear that if their employer or family members found out they were in counseling, they'd be subject to humiliation and serious repercussions. Blacks, in times of adversity or emotional turmoil, are usually told simply to "get yourself together and just don't think about it." Or, as Johnathan's father told him when he was lamenting his failed relationship, "Just go out and find another woman. She's not the only fish in the sea."

Privately, in the past, when we heard or read about whites who'd taken their own lives, we were likely to think of them as weak and crazy, dumb and foolish, because we assumed they had everything to live for. But Johnathan's parents also believed their son had everything to live for!

TERESSA RECALLS feeling uneasy when Johnathan didn't arrive for their traditional Saturday breakfast together and, most uncharacteristically, didn't call to say he couldn't make it. She drove to his house and saw his car parked, so she went up to the door and peeked in the window. She saw his bare foot and remembers screaming because, from the color of the foot and his lack of response to her pounding on the door, she knew at once he was dead. As she entered the house and approached his body, she saw blood oozing from his head. The gun she'd given him the previous Christmas lay loosely in his hand.

She remembers kissing her dead son and asking, "Why did you do this?" From that moment on total chaos prevailed. John went into severe shock; Johnathan's fellow officers wept openly upon hearing the news; friends and family rushed from near and far to be at the Statens' side.

AFRICAN AMERICANS still don't really understand how to grieve for a loved one who takes his own life. Shock, anger, guilt, humiliation, disbelief, regret, blame, and confusion descend upon the mourners in no particular order as they are swept along on a roller coaster of grief and emotion. Most people who take their own lives simply want to end their mental and emotional suffering. They don't want to hurt their loved ones, but they simply can't endure the pain any longer. In spite of this, however, it's sad but true that oftentimes, when blacks talk to the family of a suicide victim, they refer to the tragedy as an act of total selfishness. Such comments can only serve to compound the grieving experience as the family wrestles with this distorted view of their loved one and struggles to come to some understanding of the reasons for his or her act.

And too often the answer to the question "Why?" is buried with the victim. Unlike whites, most African American suicide victims don't leave a note of explanation or apology, and this lack of explanation makes it even more difficult for the survivors to engage in healthy mourning.

Grievers must understand that their own pain will be prolonged and that they need to seek professional counseling as soon as possible. The guilt and confusion can sometimes seem overwhelming as survivors consider what they might have done to prevent the suicide. But gradually these what-ifs will subside and mourners will eventually be able to come to terms with the act and find inner peace. Finding a support group where they can share their feelings and learn that they are not alone can go a long way toward helping that process.

There is one particularly unfortunate impediment to healing for some people that needs to be addressed. Because of their religious beliefs, coupled with the admonishment of the Sixth Commandment, "Thou shalt not kill," many African Americans believe that suicide is a sin and that those who take their own life will, therefore, be denied entry into heaven. As a result, these mourners grieve deeply over the thought that their loved one will be condemned to everlasting damnation. In counseling, I remind people that their loved one's decision to die should not be allowed to invalidate all the positive aspects of his or her life. I encourage them to remember that God is all-merciful and, whatever act we may have committed, by His grace, we will be forgiven. And I would counsel my fellow African American ministers to proclaim the love of God rather than His wrath when comforting grievers of a suicide.

I must also, however, caution mourners not to go to the other extreme and glorify the deceased. This is often a temptation, particularly when the victim was young. But, not only would the survivor then be recreating the dead and so mourning a stranger, he or she might also, inadvertently, by romanticizing or glorifying the one who died, be influencing other young people contemplating suicide to duplicate the act.

As much as possible, we should try to mourn the suicide death as we would a death from any other cause. Some African Americans seem to feel obligated to mourn forever and are unable to accept the fact that their loved one *chose* to die. These people must try to bless the memory of the deceased and acknowledge that his or her life is over. Once they are able to do that, they will have taken the first giant step toward recovery.

SINCE JOHNATHAN'S death in 1992, John and Teressa Staten have spoken to groups of suicide mourners, and Teressa has self-published a booklet describing the warning signs of a potential suicide, especially among those in law enforcement. They have also established a memorial fund in Johnathan's name to aid the Black Child and Family Institute for Enrichment Activities for Children in the housing complex where he worked, and they have helped other local charities. Although his death put a strain on their marriage for a short time, they became one another's main source of support during the most intense stage of their grieving. Both parents received extensive counseling and therapy, and they are now able to take comfort in their knowledge that, despite his having chosen to die, he loved them and knew they loved him. He left a legacy of love, caring, and sharing, and will be remembered for his sensitivity to the plight of young black people as well as his compassion for the elderly.

When Johnathan's mother approached his lifeless body seated in a recliner, she saw his Bible open in his lap, turned to one of his favorite passages, which reads in part, "...look not at things which are seen, but at the things which are not seen, for the things which are seen are temporal; but the things which are not seen are eternal." (2 Cor. 4:18, KJV) Perhaps this was also his philosophy of life...and death.

Teressa Staten has taken some hard lessons from the tragedy of her son's suicide and has been kind enough to allow me to share some of what she's learned, in the hope that it will be of help to others.

- *Do not expect quick relief from your pain.* Do cry, scream, exercise, talk with friends, seek professional help—whatever provides relief from your pain.
- *Accept and allow friends and relatives who sincerely care to do*

things for and with you. But be wary of those who might want to exploit your grief to feed their own egos or sense of righteousness.

- *Remember that other members of your family are also in pain.* While it is extremely important that you take care of your-self, do try to keep on expressing your support and con-cern for other family members.
- *Know that you* will *blame others and question yourself regarding what might have been done to prevent the suicide.* The con-fusion regarding the whys and what-ifs of suicide will eventually fade, but expect it to linger for some time.
- *Take time for yourself.* If possible, take time off from your job. Don't expect that you will be able to function normally for a while.
- *Accept and understand that you will see the world differently.* Previous concerns may now seem insignificant. The choices you make about what to do with your life will probably change, and you'll find it easier to say no to requests you may previously have felt an obligation to honor.
- *Join a support group, pray, or meditate daily.*
- *Know that time will be your best healer.*

✺

LESSONS IN HEALING

- Always remember that no mode of death is any more or less worthy of grief, and, no matter the cause, mourn your loved one without shame or blame.
- Be kind and gentle with yourself, and remember that if you've lost a loved one to an "unspeakable death," you may be mourning on several levels at once.
- Try to find a support group for people who've experienced the same kind of loss. There are groups for suicide survivors as well as those for parents of AIDS victims.
- If you're offering words of comfort to the family of a suicide, please try to be sensitive to their own mixed emotions about the manner in which their loved one died.

HEALING WORDS

I cannot allow negative thoughts to invade my thinking process. I now concentrate on clearing and cleansing my mind of past regrets, painful memories, and hostile, hidden secrets. Today I release all doubts and fears, and my thoughts will soar like a pure dove in flight, to heights of grace, and reach the high and higher mind of the Almighty.

※

NINE

Recreating the Dead

"Don't make me over."

Personalizing and anthropomorphizing the life-after-death experience has a particularly long, rich history among African Americans who, during slavery, sang of "putting on my robe in glory" while they toiled, wearing tattered clothing, in their masters' field, or rejoiced in the thought that "some glad morning when this life is over, I'll fly away."

This view of heaven as a personal home-away-from-home is made particularly vivid in the classic black movie *Cabin in the Sky*, in which Ethel Waters and Eddie Rochester portray their vision of the heavenly little love nest where they will live happily ever after their death.

Even the funeral programs upon which we place so much emphasis often include a farewell message intended to pro-

vide comfort in the form of a poem, song, or phrase that reflects the sentiments of the deceased for the surviving family.
One such popular poem says:

> When I must leave you for a while,
> Please do not grieve, and shed wild tears
> And hug your sorrow to you through the years.
> But start out bravely with a gallant smile,
> And for my sake, and in my name
> Live on and do all things the same.
> Feed not your loneliness on empty days,
> But fill each waking hour in useful ways.
> Reach out your hand in comfort and cheer,
> And I, in turn, will comfort you and hold you near.
> And never, never be afraid to die,
> For I am waiting for you in the sky.

Expressions such as these are intended to reinforce the notion that separation by death is only temporary, and thus to
provide hope and expectation of everlasting togetherness. For
African Americans, they paint a picture of another, better
world awaiting us as a reward after death.

• • •

PERHAPS AS an adjunct to this vision of an alternate universe, we also have a tendency to "recreate" the dead by erasing or excusing any unacceptable characteristics or behavior. "He wasn't really mean," we might say, "he just had a bad temper if you messed with him." Or, "She never meant to hurt anyone's feelings; she just said whatever was on her mind." For if we are to believe that our loved one is going to "heaven" (where we will follow and be reunited), then mustn't we also believe that he or she was a "good" person?

Our African American history and heritage have reinforced our need to believe in this vision of a concrete life-after-death that is a kind of mirror image of our life on earth, but with all the flaws, injustices, and burdens removed. It's important, however, that we learn to love and cherish our deceased loved ones as they were, not in some revised, infinitely perfected version, because once we have recreated the dead, we are, inevitably, mourning a stranger. In this context, I recall one particularly salient comment made by the eighty-year-old uncle of my cousin about a deceased relative: "He was a no-good SOB in life, and now he's just a dead SOB!"

There's also the story told of the funeral at which speaker after speaker extolled the wonderful attributes of the deceased until one elderly woman got out of her seat and approached the casket. When asked the reason for this unorthodox behavior, she simply replied, "I wanted to see who they were talking about, 'cause they sure didn't know the same man I knew."

AND IF SURVIVORS recreate the personalities of the dead, African American morticians are often asked to work miracles on the physical appearance of the deceased for purposes of public viewing at the funeral. They are asked to make the unattractive look beautiful, to turn frowns into smiles, and to make the deceased (regardless of his or her known wickedness) appear to be at peace. Such requests, however, are really just attempts on the part of the family to delude themselves into believing that in death the deceased can become something he was not in life.

In addition, obituaries are masterfully composed to recreate the life of the deceased by exaggerating his or her life achievements and exclaiming upon nonexistent virtues. Almost all these obituaries list a "host of relatives and friends" who mourn the loss of the departed when, in fact, this "host" of mourners is conspicuously absent from the funeral. And many African Americans go deeply into debt for these funerals because they are trying to convey the high level of love and esteem they held for the dead when, in fact, others might consider him or her unworthy of such lavish expenditure.

The words of an old black blues song say, "I'll be glad when you're dead, you rascal you," and some folks actually do rejoice at the departure of such a person because they refuse to take part in the recreation of the "dead rascal."

THE STORIES of two different women I've met in counseling provide particularly vivid examples of the ways in which this tendency to recreate a deceased loved one as we would have wanted him (or her) to be can hurt the survivor and actually prevent or retard completion of the healing process.

Angie came into counseling to confront her confusion about how she should grieve for her departed twenty-seven-year-old son, Ty. He'd been a rebel all his life and had caused her living grief prior to his death. Ty was shot to death by a rival for his girlfriend's affections, and Angie felt guilty because she was actually relieved by his death. She was almost glad he was dead, and yet she was also trying to explain (to herself) the reasons for his bad behavior. "He really wasn't that bad, after all. There are a lot of young guys just like him. I just let him get on my nerves," she sighed. She believed that Ty had loved his girlfriend, Lois, but, in retrospect, she didn't

think Lois was "good for him" because she knew he was jeal,
ous and "did things to make him go off."

In fact, both to assuage her guilt and to recreate his im,
age after death, Angie had gone beyond her budget to give
Ty an extravagant funeral. And, despite the fact that he had
lived in jeans, T,shirts, and sneakers, she made sure he was
laid out in a conservative suit and tie. He'd worn his hair in
braids, but she'd had the mortician cut them off. Angie was
proud that for once he looked good (at least to her), and that
this was the way she could now remember him. But his
friends commented afterward that he "didn't look like him,
self."

IT'S IMPORTANT in grief therapy to have a good, clear view
of the true nature of the deceased, and to see the various
sides of his or her personality, because not everybody knows
the same person or sees him in the same way, and, as a result,
different people grieve differently over the loss of the same
person.

Angie's grief as a mother stood in stark contrast to the
grief of Ty's friends, who mourned him as a fallen comrade,
one who'd died while standing his ground for his woman.
They recreated him as a warrior, not a rejected lover with a

bruised ego. They saw him as a man and not as an abusive monster, which is what Lois had told the police he was.

His grandmother, Bertha, on the other hand, mourned the fact that others didn't seem to understand Ty's "high-strung" personality, which she believed he'd inherited from his "no-good father."

Angie loved her son, but she also recognized his flaws, and she was shocked when she realized, after his death, that he'd become more popular dead than when he was alive. Neighbors who'd complained about his behavior now spoke of him in glowing terms, and they all agreed that he hadn't deserved to die as he did.

Although many people find this difficult, it's important to separate *who* a person was from *the way* he was. Ty, for example, was not violent by nature but could become extremely violent in certain situations, such as when he was aggravated. "Love the sinner but hate the sin" is how some black folks describe their emotions about the loss of a controversial loved one.

IN THERAPY, Angie spoke candidly about her relationship with her son, admitting that they had never expressed love for one another. Ty's obituary, however, spoke of her as his "loving mother," and his siblings were referred to as "devoted family members." Angie's daughters reminded her that they were not close to their brother and didn't even *like* him *or* his lifestyle. Yet in death they were viewed as a close family.

Angie felt like a hypocrite in mourning because she realized that the son Ty was and the son she'd memorialized were not the same person. For whom should she grieve? For the son he was or the son she'd wanted him to be?

For several sessions, I allowed her to do most of the talking. She needed to express her feelings before she could accept her son's life as it actually was. She had to entertain the meaning of unconditional love. She had to learn how to love *in spite of* her personal disappointment at the way Ty had chosen to live his life. And she then had to face her own feelings of failure as a mother.

She pondered what she might not have done for her son, whom she now loved more in death than she had in life. Although she'd been relieved by Ty's death, she'd wanted to create some redemption for his "wicked ways." She didn't want to forget him, but she also didn't want to remember the negative things about him. To accomplish this unrealistic goal, she'd felt she had to recreate her son.

After several meetings, Angie began to accept the fact that Ty had lived his life as he'd seen fit. After all, it was his life and his choice to live as he did. I counseled her to try to separate Ty's behavior from Ty as a person. Other members of the group spoke about their own needs to forgive and be forgiven by their departed loved ones, and Angie was able to identify with that aspect of the healing process. She was able to obtain some sense of relief by releasing her guilt and forgiving Ty for the grief he had caused her.

In the Christian faith, especially around Easter, we recall the words uttered by Christ in His dying hour: "Father, forgive them, for they know not what they do." (Luke 23:34, KJV) Christ was rejected by those He loved, and persecuted by many He helped, yet He prayed for them and forgave them their faults. His words also give mourners the power and permission to forgive the errors of loved ones whose actions may have caused them pain, suffering, sadness, and grief.

Angie found consolation in spiritually conveying to Ty her love and forgiveness, as well as her newfound insight into him as a person and her own complicated son. She visited his grave and "talked" to him, and she said she felt that their spirits connected druing these visits. On one such gravesite visit, she said, she actually felt that Ty loved her and knew she loved him without reservation. After that experience, she was able to move on with her life.

• • •

THE SECOND story I'd like to share with you involves Jewel, a buxom fifty-five-year-old widow whose husband, Calvin, had died after a brief battle with prostate cancer. Calvin was seven years her junior, and they had been married nine years. It was the second marriage for them both, and their friends and family often wondered how they got together because they seemed to have so little in common. She loved church and he loved to party; she saved money and he spent it; he drank excessively and was a total embarrassment to her at social gatherings. He groped younger women in her presence and was known to have "other women."

When Calvin died, Jewel portrayed him as the greatest man on earth. His flirting became "just being friendly to everybody"; his partying was his way of being sociable. The other women? Well, "everybody loved my Calvin," Jewel said with a shrug.

Although he didn't attend church, Jewel had a large church funeral for him. She personally undertook the task of writing his obituary and recreating his tainted legacy. She referred to him as "loving and kind in all his ways" and wrote of his affection for her, his wife, and his devotion to his family. She also made reference to his deep belief in God (which was news to everybody) and, because he had been in the military, she transformed him into a war hero. She selected an expensive casket and adorned the church with flowers, although everyone knew he *hated* the smell of flowers. Visitors to her home during the pre-funeral period were forced to listen to Jewel as she reinvented Calvin's "ugly ways."

AFTER THREE months of grieving, Jewel came to me for counseling. She was hurt because she felt she'd been abandoned by her family and friends. The phone calls and visits had stopped abruptly after the funeral, and now she was lonely and in deep despair. No one but her seemed to miss Calvin, and she was angry because, in her opinion, he'd been good to so many people. She'd expected emotional support from certain people who now seemed to be avoiding her, or who were insensitive to her loss.

Jewel was in total denial about Calvin's shortcomings, and for weeks she refused to discuss any of his character flaws. She was also fearful of life without Calvin and had refused to remove any of his personal belongings from their home or to rearrange any of his personal space. Her attachment to the past was both mentally and physically unhealthy. She was suffering a loss of appetite, elevated blood pressure, intense headaches, and constant bouts of crying.

Jewel craved sympathy and understanding for her plight, and she resisted any counseling that didn't include that component. She just wanted someone to say, "I know how you feel," when, in fact, very few people in her circle could comprehend why she was in such deep grief, considering the way Calvin had treated her. When I asked her to describe him as a person, she softly admitted, "He had his ways." When I prodded her to discuss these ways, she slowly began to talk about how uncaring and insulting he could be (but, of course, only when he'd been drinking).

Jewel had lost her self-esteem because of the difference in their ages and her buxom appearance, and she'd compensated by inventing a flawless relationship. She now found it difficult to accept the fact that her friends believed she was lying about Calvin's virtues, and merely concluded that "they didn't know him like I did."

Jewel's behavior is a good example of how African Americans differ from other ethnic groups when it comes to grieving, for the vast majority of us do not experience all the traditional stages of grief. Anger, fear, guilt, denial, shock, depression, and regret are generally regarded as the stairway to healing, but many African Americans, like Jewel, pause indefinitely at one stage—denial. If counseling can provide passage through one particular stage of grief, often the mourner can then cope with the rest of the healing process. Jewel felt no guilt for recreating Calvin; she wasn't in a state of shock at his passing; and her anger was not at his death but at the reaction of her family and friends to his death. Her fear was not of death but of living without her loved one.

I advised her to seek immediate medical attention for her health problems, and to assist in her own emotional healing by being honest with herself and understanding toward others. No one should expect others to mourn a loss with their own degree of intensity, nor should the survivor allow herself to become an emotional drain on those who express their sympathy or concern.

Jewel, like many others, was loving a stranger she had created, which explains why she felt so disconnected from Calvin, the man she had loved, rather than simply grieving for their physical separation. Through her own actions, she had lost Calvin twice, once to the disease that took his life and again to the "new" Calvin she had invented.

It was painful for Jewel to reflect upon Calvin as he really was rather than the way she wanted him to be. But I reminded her that she had loved him in life with all his faults and shortcomings, and I counseled her to extend that same love to him in death. Jewel was finally able to accept the fact that Calvin had loved her in "his own way." And, once she began to recover from her deep grief, she went in search of a support group. Sadly, however, such groups are still not readily available for many African Americans. She finally found a group of widows whose members were predominantly white, but she discovered, to her dismay, that their main concern and conversation were about the state of their finances and how to find another mate. Disappointed, she returned to being active in the church and started her own small group of "widow women," as she affectionately calls them, who have become a source of support for one another.

Jewel finally learned she was not alone, and she was even amused to find that Calvin must have been "cloned," because all the women in the group seemed to have had a type of Calvin for a husband—and they were at last free to admit as much among their "sister widows."

CENTRAL TO the concept of unconditional love is that we learn to live and let live, and to accept people as they are. Life is a gift, not a privilege, so learn to cherish the gift of life and the sharing of life with others. When reflecting on your departed loved ones, release your personal creation of them and let their legacy stand on its own—the good, the bad, and the different drumbeat to which the deceased chose to march.

It took the late, great Sammy Davis, Jr., to remind us in song, "I've Got to Be Me."

※

LESSONS IN HEALING

- Don't mourn a stranger; learn to cherish and honor your loved ones just as they were.
- Take the opportunity to learn the meaning of *unconditional* love.
- Visit your loved one's grave, talk to him or her, and feel your spirits join.

HEALING WORDS

Today I am sending back those negative, painful, and complicated things that should not be a part of my life. I will accept and receive only good and positive energy, for this alone will bring me a victorious life.

TEN

How to Help Through the Hurt

Now unto him that is able to keep you

from falling . . .

ST. JUDE 1:24

In the 1980s there was a popular television commercial de‹
picting an elderly woman who, after a fall, lay on the floor
hollering, "I've fallen and I can't get up!" Such is the feeling
of many who have fallen emotionally after the death of a
loved one. They feel incapable of "getting up" and grieve that
no one seems to be there to help get them back on their feet.
In the black entertainment industry, concertgoers are often
urged to "give it up" for the performer, meaning that they
should clap, holler, and generally demonstrate their enthusi‹
asm and support. If we apply this term to the grieving
process, we can see that we need to help, exhort, and assist

the one in mourning, in whatever way we can, to let go of extended grieving and "give it up" in celebration of the life that was and the continued life that's yet to come.

Immediately following a death, mourners are inundated with expressions of genuine concern and offers of assistance from well-meaning friends, family, and other associates. But, as many survivors have told me, the real need for help often comes days, weeks, even months after the death, when those offers of help—genuine though they may have been—are long forgotten. And, even in those first days, people are often reluctant to "bother" the bereaved, either because they believe the grievers need time alone to "get themselves together" or because they simply don't know what type of help they can render.

To complicate matters further, it's sometimes difficult for well-meaning friends and family to determine whether or not their efforts to reach out are actually appreciated, because many mourners give the impression that they really *would* prefer to be left alone. But members of the survivor's "support team" need to bear in mind that the griever is probably confused and sad, and may be unable to determine or articulate what he or she really wants or needs.

· · ·

TRADITIONALLY, blacks will "check on you to see how you're doing" but will offer little in the way of actually helping to do what needs to be done. Many mourners, however, require just that little push or offer of a helping hand to take care of the business they need to complete after a loved one's death. Sometimes all that's required might be driving or accompanying them to see a lawyer or the funeral director or to the bank. Sometimes just sharing a meal is all that's needed to get them back on track.

Mourners, on the other hand, ought to understand that they should never hesitate to ask for assistance. We are a powerful people, not destined to perish under the weight of life's challenges, but sometimes, in the face of death, we temporarily lose that power. We must remember, however, that anything we've merely lost can also be recovered. "Seek and ye shall find." And if we need help finding what we've temporarily mislaid, we must remember to reach out to those closest to us and ask for what we need.

African Americans tend to mistrust the aid offered by agencies and organized help groups because of what they perceive as an impersonal approach to their very personal suffering. As a result, we are even more dependent on friends and family. Often the person who will be most understanding of our need is one who has healed from a similar loss and can, therefore, not only share our pain, but also assure us that it will eventually abate. When the time comes, for example, to discard the deceased's clothing and other possessions, a friend to share the task can provide both emotional and practical support. This is a time when memories surface and tears often flow, but if there's someone there to help, the tears can turn to shared laughter when happy times come to mind.

Sometimes, before embarking on unfinished business, the survivor simply needs to talk to someone, not necessarily for advice, but just to vent his or her fears and frustrations. Or, there may be papers to be filed, and, in his or her heightened emotional state, the griever may be too upset to complete the task on his or her own. A friend can help! If there are children involved, a close family friend or relative can perform a twofold good service by taking them on an outing that will at once relieve the mourner of responsibility for a time and also provide the young ones with a respite from the house of mourning.

WHEN A death occurs suddenly, unexpectedly, or in extraordinary circumstances, those closest to the victim may require special help. Particularly if there was an accident or if the death occurred outside the home, a friend might be able to intervene with an emergency room physician or the police to ascertain details and convey them to the survivor in a sensitive and caring manner. A neighbor or relative might accompany the immediate family to see the authorities, if necessary, provide transportation, or simply make it his or her business to "be there" for the bereaved, who well might be utterly confused and feel unable to cope.

I personally knew a forty-year-old man who was killed in an auto accident. With him at the time was a woman, unknown to his wife, who also perished. It was painful for the man's widow that her "so-called friends," as she put it, felt awkward being in her presence because, as one said, "What do you say in that kind of situation? What can I do for her?" I'm here to say that, first of all, you can offer comfort and understanding. You can let the survivor know that you're aware how difficult this time must be for her, and that, as a friend, you'll be there to help her weather the storm.

Mourning is a passage one must go through no matter the circumstances of the death, and if those circumstances were difficult, that's all the more reason for the mourner to need the comfort and loving support of family and friends.

ONE KIND of sorrow that still rarely evokes the kind of understanding and sympathy it deserves is the grief so many of us experience upon losing a beloved pet. African Americans, in recent years, have joined other ethnic groups in developing strong bonds with our animal companions. Dogs are no longer considered simply canine protectors or watchdogs. Cats are no longer just a form of four-footed "rodent patrol." Rather, our pooches and pussies are members of the family, indulged with special diets, groomings, toys, and treats. But even now, few blacks are truly sensitive to the grief a pet owner feels when one of these animals dies. Not only do pet owners seldom receive any real degree of sympathy for their loss, but they are also deprived of the social ritual of farewell that is provided by the ceremonies surrounding human deaths.

It was again my colleague Dr. Blount who introduced me to the true depths of this kind of mourning when she invited me to participate in a pet-grief seminar. At first I was amused, but then I flashed back to my own childhood experience with the death of Tommy the cat, and I understood how serious this kind of grieving could be.

One elderly woman who attended the seminar spoke of her dog, Duke, who had died at the age of fourteen. Duke, she said, had been her whole life. She'd cried when he lost his agility and then his eyesight. "Miss Mildred" described their taking walks together, watching TV together, even eating together. Duke slept at the foot of her bed, warming her feet with his body on cold nights, and she swore he "didn't know he was a dog." When he became incurably ill, she'd made the most difficult decision of her life when she authorized the vet to put Duke to sleep because she could no longer stand to watch his suffering. She rubbed his body while the doctor administered the injection, comforting him while he was dying and telling him how much she loved him. She didn't regret her decision, but wished she'd had the money to bury him in a "nice" pet cemetery.

It saddened Miss Mildred even more that other folks thought she was crazy to "carry on" so about a dog. People offered to get her a "replacement" from the pound, but to her Duke was not replaceable. He'd been her friend and her companion, and the bond between them was unbreakable, even in death.

FRIENDS CARE about friends, and when a friend is affected by a loss of any kind, their grief is worthy of sympathy and attention. We as a people should grieve for and with those of us who are living with losses of all kinds that many of us could not bear. If we learn to assist those who are attempting to rebuild their lives, we will be rewarded by the sense of satisfaction attained by providing the solace that helps the heal-ing to begin.

We're accustomed to losses, and we live with those losses. But death is always the ultimate loss, and in recent years blacks seem convinced that our people are dying in greater numbers than ever before. Or, as one church lady put it, "As soon as you get over one death, here comes another." And, perhaps most sadly of all, our children are being traumatized by having to learn, at far too early an age, about the fragility of life and the finality of death.

We need to seek the help of those who are able to see be-yond the veil of life's losses and show us that it is possible to live after the death of a loved one without bitterness or despair. We must be committed to helping mourners re-energize themselves from within and resume their participa-tion in life. And the mourners themselves must also try to understand that their life still has a purpose. Black elders through the ages have told us that "The Lord helps those who help themselves" and "If you make one step, He'll make two." If we start with the *desire* to heal, and maintain our faith in God, He will provide the help we need.

One who needed a push, whether from the Lord or from an understanding friend, was Dexter, a sixty-five-year-old man who came to me distraught over the deaths of his wife and two children. Dexter was bereft and had no desire to go on without his loved ones. His wife had died of kidney failure, his son had been killed in a car accident, and his daughter had succumbed to cancer. His two sisters were also dead, he had few friends, and he was alone and miserable.

His typical day was to get up in the morning, eat "a little something," watch television, go to the store, read the paper, pay bills, take care of his few chores, watch more television, and go to bed. Dexter said he was a "family man" and a very private person, and I could see that he was on the brink of clinical depression. He'd lost his spiritual connection, and although he still professed belief in God, he didn't pray or attend church because he'd concluded that God didn't hear his prayers, or else his wife, for whose healing he'd prayed earnestly, would still be alive.

Dexter had come into my office "just to talk," and listening to him was, at the time, the greatest gift I could give. After several sessions, I suggested that he visit his neighborhood senior citizens center, where he'd find a group of peers with whom he could socialize. The center also had a lunch program, which gave people the opportunity to share a meal rather than eating in solitude. Later, Dexter told me that when he was first asked to say the grace before the meal and burst into tears, the others in the group had given him no opportunity to be embarrassed, but had assured him they un-derstood what he was feeling.

After that day, he never felt alone. His phone began to ring, and he started to receive invitations to various func-tions. Two months later, Dexter was smiling and said he felt much better. He was attending church with a "widow woman" whose company he enjoyed, and he said he'd finally "taken his burdens to the Lord." His woman friend had helped him to realize that his wife and other loved ones were at peace and wouldn't want him to be unhappy. Eventually, he made friends with some of the men in the group with whom he did "guy things," and before long he was helping a new-comer to the center who had also lost his wife.

For the first time in a long time Dexter's life had mean-ing and purpose. He was finally able to celebrate the life he'd shared with his family, and he began to realize he was blessed to still have his health and a sound mind.

THE LESSON in Dexter's story is that even if you are in a fallen state, you should never be afraid to ask for help or to accept it when it's offered. Don't transfer your dependency to those who assist you, but find ways to reciprocate with small acts of kindness. Then, when you recover—and you will, because, as long as you are alive you are not without inner strength—strive to be a source of strength for others.

❊

LESSONS IN HEALING

- Never feel that "there's nothing I can do." No matter what the situation, simply being present will provide welcome support to the griever.
- Practical help is always appreciated, so: answer the telephone, keep track of gifts of food and flowers, move into the kitchen and wash the dishes—and don't expect to be thanked by those who are so distracted by their grief that they may not even be aware of what you're doing.
- Understand that all kinds of loss are equally deserving of grief, and never disparage the depth of someone else's mourning simply because you might not understand it yourself.

HEALING WORDS

Have I lost my sensitivity to the pain and suffering of others? My body, mind, and soul need to be restored to a higher level of thinking, believing, and loving. I now reclaim my loss according to the promise of the Psalmist, "He restoreth my Soul!"

※

ELEVEN

Seasons of Grief, or The End Is Just the Beginning

But this one thing I do, forgetting those things
which are behind and reaching forth unto those
things which are before . . .

PHILIPPIANS 3:13

All life is comprised of varying seasons and cycles of time, and each requires that we adapt to some kind of change. We might have our personal preferences, but somehow we all make it through seasons of storms, blistering heat, and the cold of winter.

The seasons of our lives are comprised of good times, bad times, trying times, challenging times, and, alas, times of grief and mourning, the last of which are, for many, the worst of times. We African Americans have been warned by sea‹

soned survivors of changing times that "into each life a little rain must fall," but we've also been admonished to believe that "trouble don't last always." In other words, it's a seasonal thing, and the season will, at some point, change. The season of shock will pass, the clouds of confusion will drift away, the emotional hurricane will subside, and the storm of pain will calm.

In the scheme of life, death is the shortest season; it occurs "in the twinkling of an eye." But our reaction to death often prevents us from progressing into the season of recovery from grief. Survivors almost immediately plunge into a state of mourning which follows a pattern similar to what psychologists have dubbed "Seasonal Affective Disorder" (S.A.D.). We experience a winter of grief, which can be accompanied by unabashed hysteria, fear of isolation, regret, and depression. We take comfort in emotional memories of festive holiday seasons, Fourth of July fireworks, and funny valentines. But the mourner must be mindful that these seasons are in the past, and the cycle of time will usher in a spring of new experiences that will bring with it a season of new beginnings.

Unfortunately, for some, the heat of their angry season is indefinitely extended as they refuse to seek refuge from their sweltering rage. Others "fall" into denial or vow to remain perpetually in their "winter of discontent." But survivors need to remember that, like all living things, we grow, flour, ish, blossom, and eventually wither, but along the way we plant seeds of joy that bring happiness into the lives of oth, ers, and those seeds were meant to be perennially reborn the following season in the hearts and minds of the loved ones we leave behind.

WHILE SERVING as the senior pastor of a large Baptist con, gregation, I was very much involved with counseling mourn, ers and showing them how to continue living life to the fullest in spite of their loss. I preached that life is but a span of divinely allotted time, and that, in our grief, we must also be grateful for the time our loved one was given and appre, ciate our own time here on earth.

I still have vivid memories of one particular member of that congregation who, each December, became depressed at the approach of her late husband's birth and death days. Sister Richards couldn't understand how anyone could expect her to enjoy and celebrate the Christmas holiday. To her, the month of December was nothing more than a reminder of the fact that her husband was no longer alive. She simply went into hibernation and spent the season in her self-created cave with only the "bread of affliction" for nourishment.

At the end of a Sunday service one December, she came to my office and asked me to pray with her because she was so despondent and desperately wanted to find a way to overcome her annual season of grief. I counseled her to use this time to release her mourning—not to forget her loved one but to enter a season of healing. I asked if she'd ever given thanks for the years she'd shared with her husband, or for her own life, health, and security. I reminded her that life ought to be celebrated, and that the Christmas season is a time of festive celebration and remembrance of the birth of Jesus Christ. And, finally, I urged her to remember that her own life wasn't over, despite her husband's death.

I encouraged her to believe that she could not only survive but blossom into beautiful new life. And, after our conversation, we joined hands and prayed together, asking God that Sister Richards's season of grieving be washed away in a shower of blessings.

Anticipate a harvest of healing . . . For in due
season we shall reap . . . if we faint not . . .

GALATIANS 6:9

•   •   •

IN LIFE, all endings are followed by new beginnings, and even the end of a journey means that one has arrived at a new destination. The same is true for those who have lost a cherished loved one: The end of mourning is the beginning of the survivor's new life.

Kenny Rogers, the wonderful country music artist, had a hit song that gave good advice: "Know when to hold and when to fold." There is not only a time to mourn; there is also a time to no longer mourn.

I can't count the number of occasions on which clients have told me, "You just don't understand; my life is over; things will never be the same." We need to dispel this myth of not understanding. I do understand. People understand. We've all been affected by death in one way or another. But what mourners need to understand is that life does go on. And while it's true that things will never be the same, they wouldn't have remained the same even if their loved one had lived.

Historically, our African American forefathers observed a period of mourning during which the widow wore black clothing and male family members wore a black armband on the sleeve of their jacket. Friends and neighbors checked on the family daily, but when the allotted thirty-day mourning period was over, the family had to get on with the business of living. Neither time nor circumstance allowed them to shut down completely. This doesn't mean they weren't grieving inwardly, but they knew they had to let go and move on. Even in grief, we must get to the point where we give up the forces that are hindering our healing.

NOTHING SIGNALS the beginning of a difficult and emotionally destructive mourning more loudly than a death that causes divisiveness within the family over funeral arrangements and distribution of the deceased's possessions.

A funeral ought to be a tribute to the departed. But, too often, it is an occasion for bitter dissension among the living, who argue over everything from details of time and place to the proper dress to the cost. Moreover, they disagree about those who should be included in the program, those who should be listed as survivors, and those who should ride in the limousine motorcade.

Such bitter experiences postpone the acceptance of death and delay the beginning of healthy grieving. Arguments like these can lead to long-term estrangement among family members at a time when no one should ever be denied the ongoing comfort of living loved ones simply because the survivors have chosen to "major in minor disagreements." It is not only disrespectful to the dead, but it is also detrimental to the healing of the living to use the death of a loved one as an excuse for petty vengeance.

"Funerals are for the living, not the dead," elderly black folks will tell you, because they are more likely to reflect the preferences of the survivors than the wishes of the dead. I recall, for example, one dear friend of mine who had always expressed his desire for a small, simple, private funeral. Because he was a prominent member of his community, his family disregarded his wishes and held a large and lengthy service replete with a number of speakers and numerous cards, letters, and other written tributes read aloud to the gathered mourners. They basked in his reflected glory, but, to my mind, their public display showed a blatant disregard for what my friend had wanted.

Luckily, it is now possible to make arrangements in advance for one's own funeral, either with an established funeral director or through an insurance policy that includes preburial planning. I believe it would be wise for people of color to take advantage of these options in order to minimize the confusion and disagreements that too often result when the deceased leaves no specific instructions.

One woman, whom I never knew in life, took the notion of leaving instructions more seriously than most. I was somewhat surprised when her family called upon me to deliver her eulogy, informing me that she'd heard me preach and had left explicit instructions for her funeral arrangements, which included my participation. She'd also made arrangements for my transportation by limousine from Philadelphia to New York City as well as for my hotel accommodations, so off I went. She'd asked that I deliver the same message as the one she'd heard me preach at a previous funeral. I didn't actually recall what that was, but I assured her family that I'd do my best.

Whenever I preach at a funeral, I try to address the living rather than the dead, providing a message of comfort as well as a challenge to look upon death as part of the process of life. In this case, when I learned that the woman's name was Dorothy, I took my cue from *The Wizard of Oz* and likened the deceased to the fictional heroine who found herself in a frightening far-off land, making many friends who helped and protected her along the way, but who, in the end, only wanted to go home.

The service was beautiful and elegant, and when I left the family presented me with a generous financial gift as well as a carefully wrapped box that, they said, Dorothy had left specifically for me. On the way home in the car I opened the box and found a pair of exquisite kid gloves along with a note from her saying how much her life had been touched by my ministry. Since it was July at the time, and one of the hottest days ever recorded, I put the gloves, box and all, in a drawer and all but forgot about them until the following winter, when I came upon them one cold day and decided to put them on. As I tried to slide my hands into those gloves, I felt something that I assumed to be paper stuffing the fingers. Imagine my surprise when I discovered that Dorothy had stuffed a hundred-dollar bill into each one! Here was a woman who knew what she wanted, and who was fortunate enough to have a family that carried out her wishes to the last detail.

BY AVOIDING the debilitating effects of family arguments at the outset, one is more likely to embark on a period of healthy mourning, without the additional trauma of negative emotional grieving.

Some people have learned to construct temporary retreats or set aside times and ways to memorialize their loss along the road to healing. They might go to a favorite place or listen to a favorite song. They find solace in visiting the burial site or holding long and intimate conversations with a photograph of their loved one (strictly in private, of course). In recent years, some blacks have chosen to wear large lapel buttons printed with a picture of the deceased. And many young people, particularly males, defy the law in order to memorialize their dead buddies by spray-painting their names and messages of eternal remembrance in glowing colors on neighborhood walls and buildings. Blacks have also joined other ethnic groups in placing poems and messages to the departed in the "in memoriam" sections of newspapers on the anniversary of a death. I personally applaud survivors who celebrate the life they have lost by making a charitable donation in the name of the dead.

I rejoice with friends and clients who arrive at the point where they can let go and feel free to give away clothing, rearrange the furniture, take a trip, sell or move from the residence they shared with their loved one, and, in general, to do whatever they deem necessary in order to begin living, without lingering guilt, in these changed circumstances.

IT IS SAD when grieving becomes a way of life and people seem to live in a state of perpetual mourning. This kind of prolonged grief is not only depressing and unhealthy, it is also alienating and isolating, because, after a while, friends, relatives, and co-workers start to realize that nothing they can say or do will help, and they begin to avoid the griever. Mourners must learn to let go gradually, little by little, day by day, or else they will be at imminent risk for a total emo-tional breakdown.

More and more, African Americans are finding them-selves having to grieve sudden and multiple losses—as the re-sult of an auto accident, a fire, or, in some cases, drive-by shootings. It's particularly difficult to accept and get over the loss of a loved one who has met an untimely death, but we must always bear in mind that no matter who died, when or how he or she died, life still goes on.

WE AS A people have always possessed the internal fortitude to come through struggles or hard times with renewed strength and invigorating optimism, and these are the very qualities that can also help us in times of grief. "Seek and ye shall find," Jesus advised in Matthew 7:7 (KJV), but many who grieve do not see themselves as living a happy life after the death of a loved one, and so they do not "seek" the road to a new beginning.

While the aftereffects of death are undeniably over-

whelming to the survivor, every griever must seek to understand that his or her future life need not be either dull or un-
fulfilling. Too many people make the mistake of equating
happiness with the bond they shared with the deceased, but
no one's happiness should be based solely on his or her relationship with another person. True happiness is achieved
through our ability to adjust to change and seek inner peace.
And if in life you shared true love, that love will never be di-
minished simply because you have embarked on a new life. It
will always be pleasant and comforting to recall, a source of
strength as you move on and "seek" to enjoy life rather than
simply enduring the balance of your days.

REMEMBER THE inspiring words of the Baptist church song,
"Each victory will help you some other to win," and strive to
end your state of confusion. Not only is it imperative to let
go, it is also possible actually to become a better person after
experiencing the sorrow of death. Do not, I say, allow death
to destroy your hopes and dreams for the future; rather, anticipate with joy the dawning of each new day and see it as
one more step on the road to total recovery.

Healing and growth begin in the mind. Remember this

as you recall that when Jesus performed miracles of healing while on earth, he first asked each person one question: "Wilt thou be made whole?" And only when the answer was in the affirmative did the miracle take place. To be completely whole and lead a wholesome life after losing a loved one, the griever must *want* to heal and should not waste precious emotional energy in futile attempts to rationalize or justify the death. Mourners must get to the point where they are willing to give up those things that are hindrances to healing, which means refusing to grieve what might have, could have, or should have been.

Accept the challenge to complete the business of unfinished grieving without self-imposed complications, such as the fear of what your future will be without the departed. In counseling I've found that, after a period of time, my clients are no longer mourning the death of someone dear, but are actually grieving the changes they themselves will have to face. Their extended mourning allows them to stop functioning in the real world and, at least for a period of time, to keep living in the past. But refusing to let go of the past, and of the one they've lost, is, in a way, a form of self-punishment, because the one who is dead is beyond pain and suffering and can no longer offer solace to the living. Do not delay setting foot on the path to recovery. It's important to start, as soon as is possible, adjusting to life in the present.

THE GRIEF that results from attachment to the deceased must be allowed to diminish with time. I was surprised when, some years ago, the white co-worker of a woman who had died came to me for counseling. She had worked side by side with this woman for nine years and, although they didn't socialize outside the workplace, they'd developed a close office friendship and had confided in one another about certain aspects of their private lives. My client's attachment to the departed was deeper than she'd realized, and she was having difficulty releasing her friend. She said she couldn't glance over at the friend's desk or even eat her lunch without sinking into a state of grief and depression. She kept reliving the times they'd spent together and the confidences they'd shared.

Listening to her, I realized how tenaciously people cling to the familiar and grieve the loss of its comfort. By way of explaining her emotional predicament, I reminded my client of the song, "I've Grown Accustomed to Her Face..." We miss those with whom we've developed that bond of familiarity, knowing exactly what they'd think or say in any given situation, and it's a bond that can develop not only between soul mates but also in far less intimate relationships, such as the one between these two office mates.

There's no mystery involved here. People grow accustomed to the structure of a relationship. They're fearful of letting go, and even more fearful of finding a replacement, so they cling to the security of what was familiar.

MANY PEOPLE don't think they're emotionally capable of relinquishing their old ways for a new or different way of life without the physical presence of the deceased. Although we as a people have, throughout our history, adapted to many kinds of change, we often resist the change that is forced upon us by death, which means we run the risk of getting stuck in a state of perpetual grief. Death brings any number of unwelcome, unanticipated changes, but we must learn to overcome our fear of change. Everything, after all, is in a state of constant change. Times change, people change, and, believe it or not, even you, the survivor, will change.

All this change can be positive if you allow it to evolve gradually and naturally. "Go with the flow," black folks used to say, or, in the parlance of street-wise survivors, "Take a lickin' and keep on tickin'."

In times of trouble and grief, people of color have always

found the strength to let go of fear and replace it with faith. African Americans, traditionally, have been sustained by their religious and spiritual beliefs. When we internalize our trust in God, our faith will not waver, even when life is disrupted by death.

It's essential that we do not grieve without hope for and belief in a new and perhaps better life for ourselves. We must let go of our dependence on the deceased and look to ourselves to do for ourselves. Many people are fearful of letting go because, as they say, the deceased "did everything," and they have no idea how to function independently. These people must be assured and have faith that life will teach them how to stand, even if they have to stand alone. Our covenant with God is renewed on a day-to-day basis, as is affirmed in the biblical passage commonly known as "The Lord's Prayer." Matthew 6:11 (KJV) asks the Lord to "Give us this day our daily bread," and we must believe that bread will be provided. Be it the "bread" of strength, courage, comfort, peace, love, or joy, our daily needs will be met.

Most of us will always feel connected to a loved one, even after death, but we must be mindful that this connection doesn't prevent us from accepting death as life's final act. Letting go does not mean erasing the memory of our loved one from our mind. It does, however, mean that by letting go of active grieving, we allow new depth of meaning to emerge in our lives.

MOST IMPORTANT of all, we must let go of the false comfort of isolation. Too often, mourners resist and refuse all offers of consolation, and I have even known African Americans to lash out in anger at well-meant expressions of sympathy or comfort—"I don't want to hear it!" or, even more ominously, "Leave me alone!" These people misguidedly think of isolation as a way to maintain the illusion of life as it was. In fact, however, isolation only alienates us from the real comfort that can be provided by the warmth, empathy, and sympathy of loving friends and family who genuinely want to help us through our pain.

I was introduced to an extreme manifestation of this kind of self-imposed isolation when Hugh came to me for counseling at the insistence of his wife, Phyllis. Hugh had gone into total seclusion after the accident that took the life of their thirteen-year-old son, Hugh, Jr., and Phyllis knew he desperately needed help.

Hugh, Jr., had drowned while on a church group outing. He wasn't a good swimmer but had taken a dare to dive into deep water. When Hugh, Sr., learned of his son's death,

Phyllis said, "He aged ten years in ten minutes." The couple had wanted a child very badly and, after eight childless years, had been blessed with a baby son when Phyllis was thirty-six and Hugh was thirty-nine.

Hugh absolutely doted on his son and had planned "Junior's" life all the way through college and on to a career in professional basketball. Father and son attended games together, and Hugh, Sr., volunteered to coach his son's team, watching with pride as Junior's skills developed to a level that was advanced beyond his years. "That boy's good. He's going to be a pro," people said, and Hugh, Sr., basked in this vision of his son's future.

Phyllis said that her husband had refused to participate in planning the funeral and had been angry that he couldn't, literally, remain at the funeral home with his son prior to the ceremony. He lashed out at anyone who tried to sympathize with him and chose to remain in Junior's room, sitting in total darkness. In effect, he'd become an emotional zombie, wallowing in his own grief.

When the couple finally entered counseling, it had been more than a year since their son's death, and for Hugh there was still no foreseeable recovery. Phyllis had managed her grief in spite of her pain, knowing that she had to resume some semblance of a normal life. Reflecting on the son she had lost, she expressed gratitude to God for having given him to them, even for so short a time. With difficulty, and despite her sadness, she had succeeded in accepting his death. She realized, she told me, that more and more parents were outliving their children, and she found strength in knowing that she was not alone. She prayed, read books on the grieving experience, and allowed people to share in her bereavement. At times, she found herself having to console Junior's many friends, and to comfort others who had witnessed his drowning.

Hugh, on the other hand, was nowhere near processing the reality of his son's demise, and was angry that his wife had seemed to recover "so quickly." In grief management therapy, we point out that holding onto the departed should not be the griever's primary mode of expressing his love or the depth of his loss, and that releasing our loved one will lead to our own healing and recovery. Letting go of a death that seems senseless and irrational to the griever is a long and difficult process, and for some it can take years.

I tried to encourage and reassure Hugh by explaining that there is no preset timetable for recovery, and that the age of the departed should play no part in the process. Some

people are surprised by the profound grief parents experience at the loss of an infant or an unborn child, as if the short
life of the deceased should mean they grieve the less.

In group therapy, he met parents who had lost children
both older and younger than his son. What they all had in
common was not wanting to hear that their child was "in a
better place" or "with God." Such well-meant words of consolation only added to their anger and confusion. Hugh finally admitted he was angry, hurt, and just plain devastated
by the loss of the good times he'd shared with Junior and the
loss of his son's future.

Hugh and other mourners like him live in a world of as-
sumption. They assume that life as they plan it will continue
unchanged both for themselves and for those who are included in their plan. Have we not, after all, been taught from
childhood to believe that once we work out the kinks in our
plan we'll all live happily ever after?

Hugh's world—his plan—revolved around his role as a
father, and to revise that plan meant taking on a new identity, which was, for him, almost too frightening to contemplate. Letting go means reinvesting in life and developing a
conscious awareness that life in its present form has changed.
Hugh didn't know how to let go, and, what's more, he didn't
want to. He was still clinging to unfulfilled dreams and, in the

darkness, was reliving memory after memory of joyful experiences he'd shared with his son.

By the time she brought him to counseling, Phyllis was considering leaving her husband if he didn't start to "get himself together," because, as she put it, "I can't go on living with him like this." It's not unusual for African American families to fall apart when one parent or partner isolates him or herself in a state of perpetual mourning and is unable to let go of counterproductive grieving behavior. In these situations, the griever is unable to let go of the need for self-protection and seems to believe that his isolation is protecting him from painful emotions. These people need to accept the fact that pain is part of life and that experiencing the pain of loss is inevitable in one's lifetime.

I love the admonishment of seasoned black seniors who say, "Honey, let go and let God." And that's good advice, because "go is in God." While these words might be taken as nothing more than a simplistic explanation of the inexplicable, in actuality, they offer a way for us to relinquish daily tears and live out our own tomorrows.

Hugh saw that he was in danger of losing his wife if he didn't let go of his son. He worked hard to manage his grief, and, slowly but with determination, he was able to allow the healing process to begin.

I gave each parent in Hugh's therapy group a copy of this adaptation from a poem by Edgar Guest, which I found in a book written by a mother grieving the loss of her son.

A CHILD IS LOANED

I'll lend you for a little time a child of mine, He
   said. It may be months, thirteen years,
thirty-five or ninety-three. Will you till I call
Him back, take care of him for me? His charms
   will gladden you.
He'll bring frustrations that will help you grow. Yet
   his stay will
Seem far too brief, and you'll have memories as
   solace for your
grief. I cannot promise you he will stay, since all
   from earth go on. But
there are lessons taught down there I want this
   child to learn. I've
looked this wide world over in my search for
   teachers true and
from the throngs that crowd life's lanes, I have
   selected you.
Now will you give him all your love nor think the
   labor vain. Nor

hate Me when I call his flight and take him back
again?
I think I heard us answer God, "Dear Lord, thy will
be done."
For all the joy Thy child shall bring the risk of
grief we'll run. We'll
shelter him with tenderness. We'll love him while
we may. For all
the happiness we've known, forever grateful stay.
Should his flight
be called much sooner than we've planned, we'll
brave the bitter
grief that comes and try to understand.

As a final word, I beseech you to admit to yourself, freely and
without guilt, that you are bruised but not broken. You may
bear the scar of your grief for the rest of your life, but you
will cease to feel the pain. Do not mourn without hope that
at the end of your mourning will be a good, even better tomorrow.

THE END *is* just the beginning.

✳

LESSONS IN HEALING

- Always remember that no one's happiness can be based entirely on his or her relationship with another person.
- If you shared true love with another in life, that love will never die.
- We must "let go" of active grieving in order to welcome new meaning into our lives.
- Your life *will* change, but it will be full and fulfilling—if you let it—in new ways.

HEALING WORDS

Too long I have held on to, and have been held back by, a negative controlling spirit. I realize that in order to grow, I must let go!

In addition to the organizations listed here, you can contact your church, your physician, a hospital, or a local funeral home for services that might be available in your city.

**GENERAL GRIEF COUNSELING
AND SUPPORT SERVICES**
Association for Death Education and Counseling
638 Prospect Street
Hartford, CT 06107
www.adec.org
Check their website for a grief specialist in your area.

Blount & Odum Christian Counseling Associates
5450 Wissahickon Avenue
Philadelphia, PA 19144
(215) 848·3989

Hope For Bereaved
1342 Lancaster Avenue
Syracuse, NY 13210

Precious Gems Counseling

Rita Milburn-Dobson, Executive Director

P.O. Box 27431

Philadelphia, PA 19118

(215) 409-2907

www.preciousgems.org

The Theos Foundation

(They Help Each Other Spiritually)

1301 Clark Building

717 Liberty Avenue

Pittsburgh, PA 15222

(412) 471-7779

Specialized Counseling and Support Services

American Association of Suicidology

2459 South Ash

Denver, CO 80222

www.suicidology.org

Check their website for counseling services in your local area.

1-800-suicide

(a hotline that provides telephone counseling 24/7)

Compassionate Friends

(for those who have lost children)

P.O. Box 3696

Oak Brook, IL 60522-3696

(708) 990‚0010

www.compassionatefriends.org

Check their website to find a local chapter in your area.

Families of Murder Victims

1421 Arch Street

Philadelphia, PA 19102

(215) 686‚8078

Fernside: A Center for Grieving Children

P.O. Box 8944

Cincinnati, OH 45208

(513) 321‚0282

Survivors of Suicide

(National Office)

184 Salem Avenue

Dayton, OH 45406

(513) 223‚9096

To Live Again

(grief counseling for widows)

139 Brookshire Plaza

Philadelphia, PA 19116

(215) 464‚4155